MY MARCH
TO TIMBUCTOO

BY

GENERAL JOFFRE

WITH A BIOGRAPHICAL INTRODUCTION BY

ERNEST DIMNET

NEW YORK

DUFFIELD & COMPANY

1915

PRINTED BY
WILLIAM CLOWES AND SONS, LIMITED,
LONDON AND BECCLES, ENGLAND.

Printing Statement:

Due to the very old age and scarcity of this book, many of the pages may be hard to read due to the blurring of the original text, possible missing pages, missing text, dark backgrounds and other issues beyond our control.

Because this is such an important and rare work, we believe it is best to reproduce this book regardless of its original condition.

Thank you for your understanding.

CONTENTS

CHAPTER I

MARCH ON TIMBUCTOO

CHAPTER II

OCCUPATION OF THE REGION

CHAPTER III

THE GEOGRAPHY OF THE REGION

CHAPTER IV

ETHNOGRAPHY

CHAPTER V

OPERATIONS AGAINST THE TOUAREG

CHAPTER VI

COMMUNICATIONS

MY
MARCH TO TIMBUCTOO

INTRODUCTION

I. JOFFRE THE SOLDIER

JOSEPH-JACQUES-CÉSAIRE JOFFRE was born
at Rivesaltes on January 12, 1852. Rivesaltes is a town of six thousand inhabitants,
six miles north of Perpignan, in the department of Pyrénées-Orientales, the most
southern of France, formed at the Revo-
lution from the province of Roussillon.
The population is different from that of the
neighbouring country extending between
Toulouse and Narbonne. The Roussillon
people are mountaineers, speaking a Catalan
dialect near akin to that spoken on the
other side of the Pyrenees. All except
very old peasants understand French, but
it is none the less true that both the

B

language and the sequestered situation of the Roussillon valleys isolate the Catalans from their neighbours in the plains. Their characteristics are quite as marked as those of a Gaelic neighbourhood in the north of Scotland might be thirty years ago. Like all the mountaineers in the south of France they are either silent and almost sullen, or over-excited; but they have much native dignity and natural elegance. A true Spanish courtesy never leaves them, even when heated and on the verge of anger.

A sister of General Joffre who recently gave to an inquirer valuable information about her parentage, says that there is a tradition in the family attributing to them a Spanish origin. The general's great-grandfather is supposed to have been a Spaniard of good birth, who left his country for political reasons, and on becoming French changed his name, which was de Gouffre to Joffre. A few hours spent at the Rivesaltes town-hall in a rapid investigation of the records would be enough to ascertain whether there is more in this tradition than the universal taste for ancestry belonging to rising families. It certainly seems unlikely that a Spaniard should have been called de Gouffre, which is as French a name as any.

The grandfather of General Joffre was in some business, and apparently he was more attentive to his affairs than to his family. He had several daughters, and late in life one son—the general's father—who was left to become what he might. He became a cooper, married, came into a little money which had been bequeathed to him by his mother, turned it to good account, and managed to rear eleven children, and at the same time to make himself the proprietor of a small estate outside the town.

This industrious artisan must have been a very different type from his own sire; he centred all his attention upon his children and their education. Of the three who survive, one is the general, another son is a *receveur des finances*—the finest class of French officials—the third is Madame Artus, who married well at Rivesaltes and never left the country. General Joffre was devoted to his father as long as the latter lived, and in true French fashion, never had a furlough but the best part of it was devoted to his people in Roussillon. He loved the simple provincial life with its monotonous but never-failing interests, and never forgot the Catalan dialect.

Joseph Joffre and his brothers were educated at the Perpignan school, a state institution of no particular renown, where the future general must have been regarded as something of a star ; he was very young for his class, very tall and very fair, and almost a prodigy for his mathematical proficiency. At the same school was also educated another Rivesaltes lad, a chum of Joffre's from infancy, who was to rise with him to the end of his career, the present General Roques, who owed to his early interest in aeronautics a celebrity which his friend might never have enjoyed if there had been no war, or if the war had been delayed only two or three years.

Young Joffre's gift for mathematics along with his father's ambitions decided the next step in his career. As soon as he had passed his *baccalauréat* it was resolved that he must try for nothing less than the École

Polytechnique. Proper masters to read with him were not at hand in Perpignan, but they might have been found at the Toulouse or Montpellier lycées. Yet Joffre was sent to Paris, where his father, or his father's advisers, were sure that he would find the very best teaching.

The boy was only fifteen and a half years old, but he must have felt the solemnity of his arrival in Paris. Paris did not mean to him what it means or has meant to so many of us—a place where life is expected to be the realisation of happy dreams—it was the magnetic centre of culture, the home of learned people, whose names were associated in his mind with school-book references to great scientific discoveries. Some of the most famous among these were proud of affixing to their signature the special distinction of filling a chair at the Ecole Polytechnique, and it was an awe-inspiring thought that two or three hundred young elect were in daily commune with such men and privileged to see genius disporting itself on a familiar blackboard. Indeed, literary fame, fascinating as it is, even represented as it was when Joffre arrived in Paris by Hugo, is little in the eyes of young specialists, compared to that of a Cauchy. The poet is apt to have disconcerting eclipses in his most brilliant displays; the scientist is nearly always in full possession of his powers. It is not surprising that the École Polytechnique should attract the ambition, but even more, the craving of talented youth for intellectual greatness. If a soothsayer had foretold the good people at Rivesaltes when young Joseph left for Paris that before he was eighteen, this representative of apparently impossible hopes, would appear forthwith on a severely picked list of a hundred and thirty-two students admitted to the École, the prediction would have left them dumb for very joy.

Joffre was the youngest cadet in the whole school, but the École Polytechnique being a military college, conducted by a general on military principles, he was not a mere student, he was a soldier on his way to being an officer. His rank almost at the top of the list gave him a right to the grade of sergeant, and the very day of his admission he found himself invested with a share of authority. There is a tradition that in spite of his tall and big frame he had difficulties in managing his turbulent comrades, and this may account for the fact that at the end of the scholastic year he was twenty ranks lower than on entering. His marks, however, maintained a high level, and except in the subjects of German, French composition, and drawing, they showed the facility and mental equilibrium which must always have been his characteristics.

The École had just broken up for the vacation when the long-expected war with Prussia became a reality. Joffre, appointed sub-lieutenant in a regiment of Engineers, was sent into one of the Paris forts. He stayed there throughout the campaign and saw little of the field operations. It is not one of the least curious paradoxes of modern warfare that, apart from two skirmishes with badly-armed Touareg, the narrative of which the reader will hear from Joffre himself, the French Generalissimo, as well as most of his German opponents, may die without having actually been in action. In

spite of this comparative inaction, or it may
be on account of it, the young officer held
the memories of the year which, until 1914,
had a right to be called the Année Terrible,
deeply impressed on his soul. When he
gave his name to a Masonic lodge, a fact
which cannot but cause some surprise to
those who realise his freedom from partisan-
ship, the lodge was called Alsace-Lorraine,
and its object probably purported to be
patriotic.[1] After the battle of the Marne
the Generalissimo sent to the troops an
order in which he expressed himself with a
warmth which his previous communications
had led no one to anticipate. This docu-
ment was concluded as follows: "As for
me if I have done any good I am rewarded
by the greatest honour that ever came to me
during my whole career, the honour of commanding men like you. It is with deep
emotion that I tender you my thanks for
what you have done: I owe to you the

[1] The reader must remember that the tendency of French
Masonry is atheistic, as appeared clearly in 1876, when the
name of the Grand Architect having been deleted from its
ritual, the Scottish Lodges forbade their members all inter-
course with French Masons.

realisation of that towards which all my energies have been continuously strained for the last four and forty years, I mean the Revanche of 1870." To say so much on the part of a man whose lifelong habit has been to say little is in itself a revelation.

The years passed; the unfledged officer ripened his notions, enlarged and simplified his professional knowledge under all sorts of climates; philosophies and policies evolved and changed in his own country and even in his immediate surroundings; sometimes there were fears of war, oftener there was a stubborn and blind certitude that peace somehow must now be eternal, but the soul of Joffre, when he was sixty as when he was nineteen, hungered after the one thing that could restore *its* peace.

After the war, Joffre, like his comrades, went back to the École Polytechnique. His father's dream, since the remarkable success of Joseph at his entrance-examination, had probably been that of most parents with such a son; the young man would go on acquitting himself brilliantly throughout his course, and on leaving the École he would have his choice of one of the much-coveted government posts offered to the most distinguished students; he would be a mining engineer with a great future, or a highly-paid inspector of the national factories. Unfortunately for his family, but fortunately for his country, Joffre did not make up for his loss of marks in the first year of his course, and on September 21, 1872, when he finally graduated, it was as a lieutenant of the Engineers, and his entrance at the Fontainebleau *École d'Application* sealed his fate as a soldier.

It appeared at first as if the rapidity of his rise in the army ought to console his friends for his comparative failure as a career-making son, for in less than four years—on April 22, 1876—he was appointed to a captaincy, but he remained a captain for thirteen long years, and such a delay is exceptional even in the French army. On the whole it was not until he was promoted to the higher grades that Joffre reappeared in his early character as a successful man.

Yet he did not settle in the routine of the military life, and there is a great deal more to say about him in this obscure period than about most officers in the same stage. It is true that he spent several years in the unexciting occupations of an Engineer, building a fort outside Paris or barracks in Brittany, and surprising some people at Montpellier, where he remained for several years at the École du Génie, by leading the easy life of a young officer in a lazy southern town; but he was barely thirty-two when, after the death of his very young wife, he applied for a mission in Indo-China.

Admiral Courbet was then at the height of his reputation as a colonial officer. This experienced reader of men appreciated Joffre, and after obtaining for him the decoration of the Legion of Honour he had him sent to Hanoï as chief of the Engineering department. It may be at that period of his life that he began to strike those who came in contact with him by the very quality which to-day seems characteristic of him, viz., a magnetic power felt in spite of a hampering slowness of speech. He was popular. After his departure from the colony the soldiers of the foreign legion who had been under his orders gave his name to a street.

General Mensier who, after Courbet's death, began to use his interest in favour of Joffre, brought him back to Paris in 1888, and evidently spoke highly of him to his immediate superiors. Shortly after his return he was promoted major and employed in the military railway service until he received an appointment as professor of fortification, not, as some people have said, at the École de Guerre, but more modestly at Fontainebleau. He was there when, in 1892, he was offered another chance of seeing colonial service ; but this time it was in Africa, in the lonely Soudan, and his job was to superintend the building of the Kayes to Bafoulabé railway. It was during his three years' stay in the Sahara that he undertook the famous expedition which "My March to Timbuctoo" relates with Cæsarean rapidity. The reader will see for himself that if the French public had had nothing else than the officer's narrative by which to imagine the difficulties and magnitude of this enterprise it might have passed unperceived. But Africa exercised unparalleled fascination at the time, and the newspapers carefully recorded all that took place in the French possessions in the Sahara. The fact is that Joffre now ceased to be the obscure Engineer he had been for twenty years, and many a newspaper reader who in July, 1914, thought that he saw the name of the Generalissimo for the first time, had in reality seen it frequently mentioned years before but had had time to forget it.

In March, 1894, Major Joffre was promoted lieutenant-colonel at Timbuctoo, and three years later, at the age of forty-five, he became a colonel. The interval had been employed in what may be regarded as one of the most remarkable works of engineering accomplished in modern times, viz. the enormous fortifications of Diego-Suarès, that bay of strange configuration in the most northern point of Madagascar. On his return to France Joffre must have felt that henceforward his career could not but run smoothly; exactly four years after being given a regiment, he was appointed a general. About the same time he married Madame Lozès, the mother of the bright-looking girls who are frequently seen riding in the Bois de Boulogne with him, and the happiest and most brilliant period of his life began.

What sort of a man had he been so far ? Among many platitudes or inflated statements about the greatness he must have possessed even when he was unknown, we hear a few discordant notes. Some people who are supposed to have lived in his familiarity say that he was lazy, others say that he was ambitious, others find fault with him for having been a gayer young fellow at Montpellier than behoved the future Generalissimo of the French army : he would sometimes sing comic songs at a café to an audience of brother officers, and that is unforgivable. All this can be summed up in saying that many people who met him in early life have been rather surprised at his eventual distinction.

This, after all, is the common lot of most great men whose development circumstances have made inherently slow, or who have had to wait a long time for favourable chances. A mathematician, an artist, a poet, whose gifts invariably appear in boyhood, take nobody by surprise. Again, it must have been easy for the people who follow the career of General Foch, for instance, who saw him hold at forty the most important chair at the *École de Guerre,* and saw him ten years later return to the same École as director and commandant, to prophesy that if a war should break out before he was sixty-five and pensioned off he would play a brilliant part in it. But in the ordinary course of life it is exceptional that a famous person's intimates foresee his future celebrity. Nobody was more astonished on hearing that George Eliot was Marian Evans than the Brays in whose house the writer had lived for years. This kind of surprise mixed up with wounded conceit has been known to leave a deposit of envy even under sincere devotion.

The charge of ambition against any man with talent enough to do something well is foolish and ought not to be discussed. The charge of laziness against a man gifted with the facility commonly accompanying genius is almost as ridiculous. As Molière's *Misanthrope* says, the time spent on a piece of work matters little ; it is the result that counts. Everybody is agreed that Joffre loves military books, and that he prefers them to every amusement, but it would have been inconceivable that he should have made at Hanoï or Kayes the careful study of German military literature, which he undoubtedly undertook later in life.

Probably most people were deceived about him by the simplicity of language which he owes partly to his modest origin and partly to his incapacity for speaking in public. A man sufficiently near the people to have preserved the spontaneity of the people, yet sufficiently intelligent or gracious to dislike talking above his company, may have the most striking trains of thought and never let the people in his intimacy suspect it.

But who can imagine that whenever anybody had the chance and the tact, even years ago, to draw out the real, if hidden, Joffre, he appeared different from what his later admirers have seen him? A single conversation with him at the time of his appointment as Generalissimo convinced that widest awake of men, M. Briand, that he was the man France wanted. After one interview, Lord Kitchener did not hesitate to speak of him, one may say before the whole world, not only as a man of genius but as a great man. Yet other people may meet him repeatedly and see nothing in him except commonplace grandfatherly kindness ; or, if asked to address half a dozen people otherwise than in the course or in the tone of familiar or business conversation, they may see him grow confused and lose his powers of expression. No doubt that when clad in a *burnous* and smoking a pipe—as somebody remembers seeing him—he sat in his tent in the Soudan, he did not deliver himself of Napoleonic utterances. Some people describe him as a man in whom such perfect equilibrium prevails that brilliance was not necessary to him, but may it not be that the brilliance was there, and that if it had had an earlier chance of showing itself it would have been as dazzling as in many

c

individuals less famous than Joffre has become ?

*   *   *   *   *

In 1901, Joffre was nominated brigadier-general, and from that time his promotion became exceptionally rapid. It is remarkable also that his superiors never appointed him to any post that might have kept him too far from Paris. He first commanded artillery at Vincennes. Four years later, he received the command of a division. The army corps to which this belonged had its headquarters at Rouen, but the division itself was quartered in Paris, and Joffre was appointed at the same time member of the Technical Engineering Commission. In 1909, he was placed at the head of the second army corps at Amiens, but once more an inspectorship of the Military Colleges made his presence in Paris at frequent intervals a matter of course. Finally, in 1910, he became a member of the Superior War Council.

The Superior War Council is the supreme organ of military authority in France, and the centre of the national defence. It consists only of eleven members, from among whom it is understood that, in case of a war, the commandants of the field armies must be chosen. The presumably most distinguished of the members is given the title of Vice-President, under the — too often ephemeral—presidency of the Minister of War, but of late years the habit has prevailed, no doubt because people felt the imminence of a crisis, of calling the Vice-President Generalissimo.

When Joffre entered the Superior Council, the Generalissimo was General Trémeau, whom ill-health compelled to resign sooner than those who knew his worth would have liked. An incident, which was never made public, and which it is useless to relate here, caused General Michal, who was appointed after him, also to resign. His successor, designated by universal esteem, could only be General Pau, a true soldier, whom the loss of an arm in 1870 did not prevent from making a remarkable career. But when the Vice-Presidency was offered to him, this General pointed out that in less than two years he would be sixty-five, and would have to retire, that the predecessors of Trémeau and Michal, Generals Brugère, Hagron and de Lacroix, had all been too short a time in office, that it was of paramount importance —this was in 1911, the year of the Agadir affair—that the Generalissimo should be young enough to leave his mark on the army, and he suggested Joffre as the likeliest man in every way. Joffre was appointed, and in a very short time whoever happened to be in contact with officers began to hear it repeated as a maxim that if war must come let it come while Joffre was at the head of the army, and his two friends, Pau and de Castlenau, worked with him.

The reasons of this increasing certitude civilians naturally did not clearly comprehend. The preparation for war which is so simple in its principles and in its chief details that a child can understand it, owes to its secrecy something as recondite as mathematics. People have gradually grown accustomed not to bother their heads about matters into which it appears useless and even inadvisable to inquire. Whereas most

Frenchmen of average education will find it easy to repeat the names of thirty out of the forty Academicians, you will hardly meet one in the most intellectual salons to whom the Superior War Council is more than the vaguest of terms, and even the Generalissimo's name may be unknown to men who read five or six newspapers every day.

Some people living in the vicinity of the rue Saint-Dominique might know that the slow-going bulky figure in a short coat and flat-brimmed tall hat they saw day after day going in or out of the War Office was General Joffre; others might meet him in the Bois, a powerful horseman accompanied by two young Amazons, and become interested on noticing the marks of respect which officers showed to him; but the public at large ignored his existence, the newspapers seldom mentioned his name, and it was not until after the battle of the Marne that reporters began to retail scraps of information about his home life in the peaceful little house which he occupies at Auteuil.

So, even people who wished to learn more

about the military situation of France, and would ask questions every time they had a chance, had to be satisfied with what they heard, viz., that all officers believed in Joffre, that a man like M. Millerand spoke of him with a sort of tender reverence, or that military critics worth the name admired the unfailing simplicity of his instructions at manœuvres. As to the work carried on at the War Office it remained as much of a sealed book as ever. Only once was it stated in some newspaper that the intention of the military authorities in case of a German attack was to carry out a defensive plan, and that the concentration of troops would be made at a considerable distance from the frontier, along a line running from Reims to Langres, or even nearer Paris.

Yet, there was a side of Joffre's action which did not partake of the same mysteriousness, and from which anybody might have deduced positive information ; I mean the legislative measures which shortly after the nomination of the Generalissimo were passed by the chamber.

The army during the past thirteen years

had suffered woefully at the hands of
politicians. The Dreyfus agitation, which
had been partly the work of idealists, ended
in mere hatred of the army on the part of
the pacificist and internationalist elements.
Not only had this hatred vented itself in
abuse which filled the organs devoted to
M. Combes or M. Clemenceau, but it had
resulted in matter-of-fact legislation destined
to place the military more and more under
the civilian authorities. The Two Year
Service law had reduced the army by a
third; the generals in the highest com-
mands no longer took precedence of the
préfets ; worse than all the rest the *préfets*
were empowered to send in, every six
months, secret notes concerning the political opinions of the officers in their territory. Even the supreme command was not
independent. The Vice-President of the
Superior War Council was, it is true, by
right the Generalissimo in case of a war, but
beside him there was a head of the staff
whose business it was to stay with the
Minister of War and to assist the latter in
the nomination of the *personnel.* This

meant that, even in critical circumstances, a civilian minister might force men of his own choosing on the Generalissimo.

The Tangier incidents in 1906 had no doubt given a salutary shock to the country, but the politicians had gone on minding their own affairs, and in fact most of the anti-militarist or anti-patriotic measures I have just mentioned were passed after 1906. The belief in everlasting peace was so deeply rooted in those unpractical minds that repeated warnings in 1908 and 1909 could not shake their security. It was only in 1911 that the popular feeling exasperated by the insolence of Germany became overwhelming, and the more sensible Radicals acknowledged that the immediate preparation for a war was now necessary.

However, it is not unlikely that Joffre, like his predecessors, might have worn out his energy over obscure technicalities, had he not found the help of a man of rare abilities and courage, the nearest approach to a statesman there is in France, M. Millerand.

M. Millerand, in the years 1892–1899, was the leader of the Socialist party, while

M. Jaurès was yet a moderate Republican
asking himself whether he would not do well
to become a violent Radical. But there was
no similarity between the two men. Jaurès
at his best was only an eloquent idealist,
whereas Millerand is a doer of deeds, craving
clarity in everything, and trying to realise
without delay what seems to him immediately possible. In 1898, M. Millerand
was chosen by M. Waldeck-Rousseau as
Minister of Commerce, and this circum-
stance was the turning-point in his life.
Before his tenure of office he had worked
for his party; the moment he became ini-
tiated in the difficulties and responsibilities
of government he appeared as a patriot, and
began to judge everything from the patriotic
standpoint. His habit had always been to
go to the root of the questions he tackled,
ask for information from the most competent
persons and pass to action the moment he
saw his way to practical resolutions. He
followed the same method as Minister of
Commerce, as Minister of Labour, and as
Minister of War. " I only know one pro-
cedure," he wrote in 1913; " the Minister of

War has the responsible chiefs at his elbow,
let him take their advice and act upon it."

The responsible chief in January, 1912,
when M. Millerand became Minister of
War in the Poincaré government, was
Joffre, and it was soon evident from the
tone of affectionate comradeship between
the two men that their conceptions tallied,
and that M. Millerand, the experienced
politician, was making it his business to
give back to France the purified army which
Joffre, Republican and Freemason as he
was, thought necessary for the safety of
the country. The results these two men
obtained in the short space of a year were
unparalleled in the history of the Third
Republic, and, in fact, may be unique in
Parliamentary history. It would be useless
to go into details, and it is enough to say
that at the beginning of 1913 the French
army had become as popular, or rather
as respected, as it had ever been, and that
the worst traces of political interference
had been banished from it. But one
especially important point ought to be
noticed. The greatest danger to the unity

indispensable in military operations was, in the opinion of Joffre, the possible opposition between the Generalissimo on one hand, and the Head of the Staff and the War Minister on the other. M. Millerand took office on the 14th January; six days later, by the 20th January, the duties of the Head of the Staff had been made over to the Generalissimo.

The characteristic difference between the action of Joffre and that of his predecessors lay in the spirit which inspired it. The generals who had come before were all men of capacity, and two of them, at least, General de Lacroix and General Trémeau, were admittedly masters of their art. But whether on account of the circumstances or because these generals lacked the divining power and the craving for action which eminently belong to Joffre, they seemed to work on an army that *might* have to fight, whereas the present Generalissimo never seemed to entertain any doubt that his army *must* fight. In 1913, Joffre delivered before the cadets of the École Polytechnique one of the two or three addresses which are all the record of his eloquence. His hearers were soldiers like himself, and he spoke to them of the only subject that ever seemed to interest him—the military preparation of the country. "To be ready," he said, "means nowadays a degree of preparation which those who conducted past wars could hardly conceive. It would be an illusion to reckon on the *impetus* of the masses, even if it were to leave behind that of the volunteers of the Revolutionary wars, unless it is helped by an organisation. To be ready means to have turned all the resources of the nation, all its intelligence, all its energy, towards the one object—victory. Everything must be foreseen, no extemporising will avail; what will be lacking at the declaration of war will remain lacking, and the least gap may cause a disaster."

The firmness of this language in a man whose incapacity to cope with words is almost proverbial, ought not to cause any surprise. The tone and rhythm of the passage I have just quoted leaves no doubt that the man who delivered it was full of a pent-up certainty which nothing could shake. This certainty did not merely concern the inevitability of a fight with Germany, which documents recent at the time, made probable within a year or two.[1] The magnetism of Joffre would not be what it is if his divination of the future had not been accompanied by faith; the Generalissimo never doubted that the preparation which he constantly recommended would be sufficient in time, and that a war with the support of England and Russia must result in the restoration of France to the rank she occupied in the world before 1870. The officers who worked with him and who spread abroad their belief in his power saw, it is true, daily proofs of his facility in mastering the numberless details attending the mobilisation of a modern army and the complicated execution of a plan involving millions of men; but the Generalissimo's fearless acceptance of his responsibilities was really the condition of his extraordinary influence. Not only soldiers living like himself in the meditation and expectation of a war, but even civilians, even

[1] *Vide The French Yellow Book* : despatches from M. Cambon, dated 6th May and 22nd November, 1913.

the Radical successors of M. Millerand at
the War Office caught the contagion of his
certitude. History will tell us whether it is
true or not that they wavered once in his
absence, but it is a fact that whenever he stood
near his presence was enough to steel them.

Some people have described Joffre as what
they are fond of calling a " Republican," that
is to say, after all, a pacificist general, one who
hates war and blood, and only submits in
fighting to an unwelcome necessity. I am
afraid that this is a short-sighted reading.
The psychology of the soldier no doubt is
not simple, it reconciles many contradic-
tions; but a man only joins the army
because war has a fascination for him, and
in his heart he longs for an occasion of
defending his country. Joffre is too much
of a soldier to be an exception; he may
resemble Turenne or Drouot, he certainly
does not resemble General André.

A true soldier, an organiser of genius, a
patriot, a man possessed of one unconquer-
able conviction and of an indomitable will;
this then was the chief who in August, 1914,
at the age of nearly sixty-three, took the

command of the French army to repel the German aggression. Compared to Bonaparte he was old and as yet had achieved little ; but modern war has ceased to be a mere art, it is a science, with so many branches that a lifetime is not too long for its mastering, and from this point of view Joffre with his clear head, his forty years of study and practice and his special genius, with the additional superiority which his three years' experience as Generalissimo gave him, could have but few rivals. Germany herself with her methodicalness, her perseverance in the long preparation of her staff, and her evident superiority in keeping her military men away from politics, could not produce a more accomplished general, and among all those whom she pitched against Joffre not one could have the latter's belief in his cause. It is no wonder, therefore, if, in spite of inconceivable difficulties, the French Generalissimo showed himself equal to the hopes of his most enthusiastic admirers in his conduct of the war.

The history of the military operations is

only a chronology, and in some parts, the first four weeks especially, it is far from being clear. Yet what we know is sufficient to warrant us in adhering to Lord Kitchener's appreciation of Joffre. It required more than ordinary generalship, it required un-paralleled energy in the man who knew that the hopes of France were centred upon him, to act with the perfect self-control which Joffre preserved through the month of August. Let it be remembered that the French public believed in immediate success, and that ninety-nine people in a hundred felt sure that if Belgium could hold on for a few days the German armies would never pass the Meuse. Now, after a few days' uncertainty between the first battle of Dinant and the battle of Charleroi, what we saw was a continuous retreat, a bodily displacement of the whole line of allied armies which suggested a landslide, until German aeroplanes were daily seen over Paris, and patrols of Uhlans began to appear in woods where Parisians take their Sunday stroll. The press showed extraordinary firmness, and so did the poorer classes;

but among the *bourgeoisie,* that is to say, the *milieu* which immediately influences politicians, there were doubts and repinings. The people who left Paris in the stampede of 28th August to 3rd September, were fast losing their faith in Joffre and his collaborators.

The Generalissimo being in contact with an army the morale of which was unimpaired, knowing exactly where he was going, and having for years considered the possibility of the happenings which seemed so distressing to others, had no reason to lose his calm. Yet he must have felt the change in the atmosphere of the country, and no matter how attentive to his plan, he could not see the invasion of almost an eighth part of France without a pang at heart. But he never showed a sign of disquietude or impatience. Day after day his official statements recorded the advance of the enemy with unflagging accuracy, until suddenly he gave the famous order which can be summed up as " Stop or Die," and checked the Germans on every part of the line.

D

Many sanguine people have since that glorious day been surprised at the cessation of the Allies' offensive, many unimaginative people have failed to see the magnitude of the fights on the Oise and the Yser in October and November, 1914, many unthinking people have been unable to realise how much it meant to have nullified the efforts of the Germans on every point where they had boasted of being sure to conquer, but nobody since the battle of the Marne has dared express or even feel disappointment. Belief in Joffre is as absolute as Joffre's belief in his men, and it may be gratifying to the Generalissimo to see confidence thus restored, but not a sign shows that he might have been staggered for one moment had it been otherwise.

The energy which Joffre displayed as a strategist he also evinces as an organiser, and in this respect he is remarkably like Lord Kitchener. After the battle of the Marne he wanted new men, new ammunitions, and a large amount of artillery: all this has been provided. Another point of a more delicate nature had to be seen to. Some

people in high positions had proved unequal
to their duties.   It is no secret that Joffre
began an extensive rehandling by having
his old collaborator Millerand reinstated in
office among men who were his political
opponents, and went on with generals and
officers of all grades—some of them his
personal friends—whom he removed as
mercilessly as the Comité de Salut Public
used to do.   Not once has any criticism of
these changes been heard.   All the generals
now in command—Dubail, Sarrail, de Langle,
Maunoury, Franchet d'Espérey, de Mau-
d'huy, de Castelnau, d'Urbal, are there
because they showed proofs of capacity in
the field.   Joffre's decision in discerning and
promoting merit belongs to a great captain.
General Foch, now his assistant and possible
substitute, did not even command an army
at the beginning of the war, while General
de Maud'huy was a plain brigadier, one in
six or seven hundred.   The Generalissimo
accepts responsibilities, but he claims the
initiative which ought to go with them.

On the whole it can be said that Joffre

has gone successfully through the most terrible ordeal that a modern soldier could face. During three years he spoke of the military preparation of France as a momentous thing, but one that could be accomplished; gradually his confidence gained all his countrymen, and he was regarded as the defender of his nation before having had one real occasion to be put to the test. The test came at last, and all that Joffre had been in time of peace he remained in face of the most terrible danger : whatever may happen he is sure of the gratitude and admiration of his country.

This is not all. Nations are judged by a few, representatives, and it is a fact that France now holds a position in the world which she did not possess at the beginning of the war. I do not mean only that her diplomatic and political prospects are improved : this may happen to other nations which have left their swords in the sheath ; I mean that she is more respected than she was ; and her human and moral value has immeasurably increased. The Frenchman appeared for a while in the eyes of a superficial world as a decadent being with more brains than will and a propensity for reckless political experiments which it was amusing to follow. The memory of hundreds of names in the history of French thought and French action, embodying at the same time perfect intellectual balance and a Roman energy, had grown dim : in the country of Descartes and Pascal, of Corneille and Molière, above all in the country of Louis IX. and Jeanne d'Arc, some people would only see brittle charm and brilliant levity. The rapid disappearance of this uneducated notion is the change for the better which I wish to imply. The whole past of France has forced itself once more on the world, and the sympathies she attracts among her allies, in neutral European countries and above all in America are based on esteem. For this Joffre is as much to be thanked as for his victorious resistance to the enemy. Whoever possesses even a slight knowledge of history must see that his qualities are those of his nation at its best, and that he is nothing else than a traditional Frenchman. History, after the apparent standstill of the

war, will resume its usual course, there will
be mutations and vicissitudes, but for
many years to come the country which
produced Joffre will be judged with refer-
ence to the moral possibilities embodied in
him, and this is no doubt what Lord
Kitchener bore in mind when he spoke of
the Generalissimo as a great man.

II. JOFFRE AS WRITER

Towards the end of 1893, Joffre was at
Kayes in the Soudan, superintending, as I
said above, the building of the railway.
Colonel Archinard, who had been so far the
superior commandant, had just left for
Europe, and during the interval between
his departure and the arrival of the first
civilian governor, M. Grodet, Colonel
Bonnier was in charge of all the operations.

Bonnier was, therefore, the superior of
Major Joffre, though his junior by four
years, and only thirty-seven years old.
This well-known, and still regretted officer,
on graduating from the École Polytechnique had joined the marines and demanded

to be employed in the Colonial service. He had hardly been two years in the Soudan when he succeeded in reaching Bamokó from Kayes, and instantly made his name famous; he was not twenty-five years old. He left the Soudan for the Tonkin in 1885, but immediately after the campaign he returned to Africa and went on with his work there until his untimely death. It was Bonnier who conceived the bold plan of extending the zone of French influence as far as Timbuctoo. The importance of this town could not be exaggerated, and had been pointed out by the only three European travellers who had reached it in the course of two centuries, the English officer Major Laing, the extraordinary French explorer Caillé—a self-taught sailor who produced an admirable narrative of his adventures—and the Hamburg traveller Barth. Timbuctoo was only a small town of eight to ten thousand inhabitants, but its situation near the curve of the Niger in the centre of the Sahara, and at the crossing of all the caravan roads made it commercially the metropolis of Central

Africa, while the purity of the Arabic spoken by its inhabitants attracted the natives of those parts as Fez attracts those of the north, while the vicinity of the Touareg tribes, the most respected for war-like power and antiquity of descent of the whole Sahara, gave it an exceptional political value.

The farthest French post in 1893 was Ségou and Timbuctoo is about 470 miles to the east. The easiest and practically the only route to it was up the Niger, and six years before Lieutenant Caron, of the navy, had succeeded in reaching its immediate neighbourhood in a gunboat; but Bonnier thought it advisable for the execution of his design, which involved something more permanent than a mere reconnoitring trip, to form two important columns which were to reach Timbuctoo by different routes. He himself was to sail up the river with a flotilla commanded by Lieutenant Boiteux, of the navy, while the column commanded by Joffre went by land, that is to say, followed the outskirts of the Niger inundations.

Bonnier started the first and arrived at Timbuctoo without much difficulty on 10th January, 1894.   But five days later he was surprised during the night by the Touareg in a village called Tacoubao and was killed with eleven of his officers. Joffre only left Ségou on 27th December, and, as was inevitable in a marshy and almost desert land, did not get to Timbuctoo till 12th February.   On the way he heard of the deplorable fate of Bonnier and his companions, and the reader will see how he managed by constant watchfulness and frequent offensive not only to avoid attacks, but practically to destroy the perpetrators of the massacre.   Shortly after his arrival, Joffre received letters recalling him to Kayes, but feeling sure that this order would promptly be revoked—which proved a correct surmise —he stayed and set about pacifying the country and fortifying the most important strategic points.   He was back at Ségou six months and a half after his departure, having established French influence in the most   important   and   most   inaccessible African district in a permanent manner, and having collected much useful information about its inhabitants. On 6th March letters received at Timbuctoo had informed him that he was raised to a Lieutenant-Colonelcy, and at the end of 1894 he was made officer of the Legion of Honour. Shortly afterwards he was recalled to France.

It was during the first months of his stay in the mother country that he was asked to write a report on his expedition. He had evidently kept a log, and had a file of the orders and letters sent or received during the expedition. He had also made notes concerning the native populations he had visited. Using his diary as a foundation, supplementing it with the official documents, and every now and then with references to what had happened after his departure, and inserting the ethnological chapters which were all ready among his papers, he produced a report which the *Revue du Génie* published in 1895, under the truly military title of *Operations of the Joffre Column before and after the taking of Timbuctoo*. A reprint of this, to-day almost impossible to procure, was circulated by MM. Berger-Levrault the well-known military publishers. It is and will probably remain the only published work of General Joffre.

* * * * *

I have never read any reports of Loti, who, as Captain Viaud, must, however, have written many. There can be little doubt that they are very different from his books. Yet I fancy that if Loti had had a chance of going to Timbuctoo as early as 1894, and when hardly half a dozen Europeans had reached the mysterious town, the report he would have been asked to write would have been a report certainly, but also a piece of literature. With his innate sense of art he would have compressed the wonderful descriptions which fascinate us through pages and pages of his works, but the descriptions would have been there all the same. An adjective placed in a certain manner, a few bare facts from an apparently matter-of-fact note-book, but used at the right moment, would have had the same effect in the report as those simple phrases artlessly repeated have in his books. We should have read a report, but our impression would have been that produced by a work of art. We should have seen the broad Niger on its way from the great solitudes; the marigots with their pools, their mud, and their grass would have haunted our imaginations; the sudden appearance on the page of a Touareg scout, motionless on his camel at the top of a hill, would have remained engraved on our memory. We should have closed the book with the usual remark: what a wonderful artist this unliterary officer is! and in our sub-consciousness another sentence would have been whispered: and how he must enjoy writing like that!

The impression left by Joffre's way of writing is so different, that it is, indeed, the very reverse. In 1875 he evidently had not even the notion of an artistic composition, and in this ultra-literary age it seems ex-traordinary. At forty-three as at eighteen, when French essay-writing was his weak point, he cared nothing for words. His life meant action, not expression, and all

his attention was centred on results. So his
report is exclusively a soldier's report,
stating with minute accuracy all the events
he thought useful to record and adding
information for which another soldier
might be grateful.

The style is everyday language, which
only its rapidity and transparency of
thought save in several places from being
tentative. Joffre is not one of those
Cæsarean narrators frequent in all armies
who, talking or writing, hit at once on the
word we want to hear; but as he never
fumbles and apparently has no suspicion
that another word might be better than
the one he uses, the effect is almost the
same. We are even glad not to be
visited, even so fleetingly, by a misgiving
that the doer of deeds feels that he tells
them well.

Now the strange result is this : We have
grown so tired of the effort of numberless
people at fine writing, and fine writing has
become so easy and so cheap that we never
miss it. Its absence surprises us at first, but
the surprise is mixed up with a comfortable

feeling, a sensation of freedom in our minds, and an at first unperceived appeal which is that of sincerity. Let the matter, under such circumstances, be interesting in itself, and we shall give ourselves up to it without any apprehension. This is what happens to the reader of Joffre. The matter which he is concerned with is absolutely pure and acts upon him without any intermediary. There are things of so subtle a charm that even the lightest touch of art makes them vanish. For instance Loti would know how effectively Arabic names would appear in his narrative, but we should know he knew it. With Joffre, who has no idea of this, the effect produced is the same as that of reality itself. The names of the tribes he meets or describes take on a strange virtue as if we heard them on the spot. Even the French officers' names scattered over a narrative from which all attempt at picturesqueness is banished produce picturesqueness. But since, in reality, picturesqueness is everywhere in the things themselves, since the Niger really flows by, and since the marigots really lie green or yellow under the white sky, and since the Touareg sentry on his camel is a daily occurrence, and the ghastly scene at Tacoubao an awful fact, we constantly see visions rising in our minds as vivid as it is possible for words to conjure. Needless to say that when there is an inborn charm in the words themselves, as sometimes happens, we enjoy it to the full. Whole volumes on the religious and pastoral tribes, living their peaceful life beside the violent Touareg, which Joffre barely enumerates, would not give us so much poetic pleasure as he does by calling them in two substantives—not adjectives—*religieux pasteurs*. But had he had any suspicion of this our pleasure would be gone.

On the whole, Joffre as a writer is—much as he is a soldier—a sort of primitive whose strength, associated with perfect simplicity, appeals directly to us. It is not saying too much that his unsophistication as a handler of words is not only refreshing but moralising, and that literary education on the bases which are unconsciously his own would be as much a tonic for a country as the example of heroic patriotism which he offers ; but this the reader will feel for himself, and it is time to conclude this too long preamble.

NOTE ON THE TRANSLATION

THE translation which follows is practically literal. Joffre has a way of visualising things to which the English language with its superior graphic power would do more justice than French. But in many instances it has appeared advisable to resist the temptation to make the *March on Timbuctoo* so idiomatic that it might no longer suggest the original text.

Arabic words used by Joffre have been left untranslated as in his text.

ERNEST DIMNET.

OPERATIONS OF THE
JOFFRE COLUMN

BEFORE AND AFTER

THE OCCUPATION OF
·TIMBUCTOO

Published with the Authorisation of the Minister
for Colonial Affairs

E

PREAMBLE

Column No. 2 was organised at Ségou by order of the commandant supérieur on 25th December, 1893, arrangement and strength as follows :

1 major ;

7 captains, 9 lieutenants or sub-lieutenants (of whom 2 were natives), 1 interpreter;

380 troops (of whom 352 were natives);

42 drivers and 662 auxiliaries (porters and servants) ;

183 horses and 18 mules.

The column required considerable quantities of millet and rice on account of its large number of horses and mules, and provisions had to be renewed frequently on the march. This sometimes retarded the advance of the column, owing to the difficulty of procuring a great quantity of grain in a poor and often hostile country. Several times the rations were reduced. However, we could always get plenty of sheep, and could increase the ration of fresh meat when other provisions were scarce.

THE MISSION OF THE COLUMN

The mission of the column was to advance on Timbuctoo by the left bank of the Niger, by way of Sansandig, Monimpébougou, Nampala, the Lake of Kabara, Soumpi and Goundam.

In the first part of the march we were to declare our authority over the country, and to send to Sokolo, to Djenné or to Sansandig, those among the village chiefs who belonged to the first two circles[1] or to Mademba fama of Sansandig, those who had not yet offered their submission in person, or who had any disagreements to be settled.

In the second part, from the Lake of Kabara to Timbuctoo, we were to take possession of the country, populated by tribes which, until then, had been independent of us, and among which, some would probably be hostile. To this end, we were to bring the chiefs of these regions to Timbuctoo, where Colonel Bonnier was going by the river for the purpose of organising the country.

[1] A circle = district.

CHAPTER I

MY MARCH TO TIMBUCTOO

FROM SÉGOU TO TÉLÉ (88 MILES)

THE 26th December was devoted to the organisation of the column, and the 27th to crossing the river at Ségou. The troops were transported in the pirogues[1] of the post. Our passage required some time because of the large number of horses, which swam across with their heads resting on the pirogues. It was 9 o'clock in the evening before all were over.

From Ségou (left bank) to Nono (50 miles) we progressed under normal conditions over a beaten track through familiar country. However, the natives of the village of Monimpébougou were so slow as to seem almost unwilling to furnish us with the produce we asked for: three tons of

[1] A long narrow canoe made from a single tree trunk,

millet and fifty sheep. It was necessary to send an armed section into the village to collect these provisions.

From Nono to Télé (88 miles) the usual road was at this time flooded. We were obliged to cross the bush over sheep trails. These trails twice led us to pools left by the overflow of the river, which was now beginning to fall. We were compelled to go around these pools, cutting our road with axes through the thickets. We reached Télé on the 8rd January, after marching for two days without having seen a single habitation.

From Télé to Oudiabé (70 miles)

From Télé a road leads directly to Soumpi, passing by the ruins of Gardio and by Diartou. This road was then entirely under water, and to take it was out of the question, although it was by far the shortest route. On the other hand, we could not skirt the inundations of the Niger, which were then falling. We should have been constantly kept away from the water by the soft mud left by the river in this region. Furthermore, as the floods spread in the valleys much further out than in the higher parts of the country, long and numerous detours would have been necessary, and the distances would have been considerably lengthened. Besides, these parts are uninhabited, and we could not have found any guide who, taking us straight from one inundation head to the next, might have avoided the many inlets and made the road as short as possible.

It was necessary, then, to take the path followed by the natives, which passes by Dioura 25 miles away, by the well of Boulavi, 22 miles further on, and ends at Oudiabé, 20 miles beyond. These three are the only places along the route where there is water.

We covered the distance from Télé to Dioura between 4.15 o'clock in the afternoon and 10.30 the next morning, with a rest of seven and a half hours in the ruins of Niarniardé, where we spent the night. In the village of Dioura there are four wells, which gave us all the water we needed.

At Boulavi there is only one well 200 feet deep which, with the means at the traveller's disposal, supplies only 15 litres of water every five minutes. Although we had arrived at 1.40 in the afternoon and did not leave till 4.15 the next morning, and though water was drawn all night, we could only give the troops and the animals a very small ration of water. As for the porters, they had had no water at all as yet ; and, to enable them to quench their thirst a little, they were left at the wells after the departure of the column.

We now crossed a desolate, nearly desert country under a burning sun. We arrived at the village of Oudiabé, in the canton of Nampala, on the 7th January, at 12.45 in the afternoon, leaving behind several stragglers exhausted with heat and thirst.

In order that all should have water in sufficient quantity and as soon as possible, the troops were divided among the villages of Oudiabé, Diavambé, N'Doudi 1, and N'Doudi 2, which each possessed an abundant well. At 3 o'clock in the afternoon all the troops were settled in camp.

We then gathered as many porters as we could find (tirailleurs who volunteered, and natives), and despatched them on the road to Boulavi to carry water to the convoy which we had left there. Five groups of porters were thus sent between 3 o'clock in the afternoon and 8 the next morning, 150 porters in all,

The convoy had left Boulavi on the 7th at 12.30 p.m., but being obliged to halt between 1.30 and 4 in the afternoon on account of the great heat, by nightfall they had only covered 6 miles. Starting again the next morning at 6.30, they were able to reach Oudiabé at 3 in the afternoon thanks to the convoys of water which they met at intervals along the road.

This scarcity of water during a long march in the intense heat fatigued the troops excessively and exhausted a considerable number of porters. Rest was necessary, so the column remained in camp until the 10th. This halt was also necessary in order to get a fresh supply of provisions, as ours were entirely consumed. The troops found sufficient grain for themselves in the villages where they were encamped. But from Oudiabé to Soumpi, the first inhabited place we were to reach, there would be six long stages, and we would, therefore, have to carry at least six days' rations, that is, nine tons of grain.

Immediately on our arrival Ibrahima Ahmady, chief of the canton of Nampala, had been called upon to furnish us with these provisions. He was the successor of El Hadj Bougouni, former chief of the country, who declared himself our enemy and openly allied himself with the Touareg tribe of the Kel-Antassar, with whom he took refuge. Ibrahima, nominated by the commandant of the circle of Sokolo, had as yet little authority over the village chiefs. After trying for 24 hours, he was obliged to acknowledge his failure to get the provisions, and asked for the aid of an armed troop to enable him to fulfil his task. A section of our tirailleurs then accompanied him to the various villages of his canton, which, at the mere sight of our soldiers, at once supplied the food we demanded.

From Oudiabé to Soumpi (113 miles)

On the 10th January the convoy was reorganised, and the troops having been sufficiently refreshed, the column broke camp at 5 in the evening. The route from Oudiabé to Soumpi passes by Diabata, Léré, Manguirma, and Diartou. The flood of the Niger, exceptionally high that year, had entirely covered the road; and while in the environs of Léré the water had commenced to fall, the level was rising when we left Diabata.

It was at Gallou that we came upon the inundations, and from this point onward we never got away from them till we reached the Lake of Tenda. The guides were not sure enough to lead us directly from one flood-head to the next. We were continually compelled to skirt the edge of the water, otherwise we should have been in danger of getting lost in the sandy desert which borders on the inundations, and also of lacking the necessary water for the men and horses.

We were compelled, therefore, to follow

a very sinuous line of march, across sandy ground planted with mimosas, generally sparse, but sometimes growing thick enough to add to the difficulties of our progress.

We arrived at Soumpi the 16th January at 8.20 in the evening, having covered 112 miles from Oudiabé.

Off the Lake of Kabara we had received the messengers of the chief of Diartou, coming to notify us of the submission of the village. We learned there that the Kel-Antassar, informed of our approach by the spies of El Hadj Bougouni, had left the country several days before.

We reached Soumpi the day following the departure of the last Touareg.

After Soumpi

Abdoulaye, chief of the villages of Soumpi, Daïbougou, Kassouna, Gamba and Diana, placed himself under our protection and consented to accompany me to Timbuctoo, there to receive the instructions which would be given him by the commandant supérieur of the Soudan. The same consent was also given by Sididio, heir of the canton of Aoussa-Katawal, which includes the five villages mentioned above, and extends from Diartou to Niodougou. This canton was at the time without a chief, both Abdoulaye and Sididio canvassing for the office. The question was to be settled at Timbuctoo. Assoumana, chief of Niodougou, was also to accompany me to that city. All the chiefs were to render us important services in our march across a country entirely unknown and almost uninhabited. The fertile lands of Aoussa, some cantons of Niafounké and Atta were then under water; the roads were impassable, and, in fact, the column, in order to reach Goundam, had to wind around the larger lakes, marching nearly always on sand, and was obliged several times to cross mountainous defiles of difficult access.

Reliable guides are necessary in crossing this country, and the chiefs whom we took with us were to assist us in finding such guides, and in checking the information they might give.

The Touareg Method of Fighting

The chiefs also gave us valuable information as to how the Touareg fight. As they fear the power of our arms, they will not molest us by day nor accept a face-to-face combat. But they will watch our advance, and try to capture soldiers, or small groups, found at a distance from the column. They will try above all to surprise us by night, when they will expect our sentinels to be off their guard.

Slaves, armed with lances, hidden behind bushes, or sometimes concealed in the branches of trees to get a better view, will be here and there in the bush. Some of them will get caught, but all the same, the Touareg will be well informed of our movements by the rest. Others mounted on swift camels will be stationed on rising ground from which they can overlook a vast expanse, and can consequently observe us from a great distance, carrying their information at once to the chiefs. The chiefs are always on horseback, and they estimate the force of a column of troops in proportion to the number of its horses.

This explains why the Touareg considered the column which went to Timbuctoo by land as being much the more important. It comprised the horses and mules of both columns—about 250 in all. This large number of animals retarded and handicapped us, owing to the immense quantity of grain necessary for its subsistence, and because it made our surveillance more difficult, but it was considered a great force by our enemies.

OUR MARCH

In order to be ready for a combat at any moment, the column marched in three files of one man or one horse each. The Spahis acted as advance and flank guards, always in connection with the main body, and at a distance varying from 110 to 880 yards, according as the ground was more or less open. Thus the troops were always in close touch with the commanding officer, the column not being too long, so that there was no danger of small groups of men getting lost and finding themselves far enough from the main body to be at the mercy of a sudden attack from a party of Touareg. As the Touareg used very few if any guns, the formation adopted enabled us to keep an effective watch.

The Camp

We always pitched our camp in the form of a square; and nearly always it was possible to set our backs to the water, which left us only three sides to guard. Several times, in fact, we set up camp on land nearly surrounded by water, in which case we had to guard one side only.

The country we now crossed contained a great many mimosas, whose thorny branches the native shepherds cut and make into fences for their cattle folds. Abandoned folds enclosed in this way are found everywhere. Also, when setting up camp, an abattis[1] of thorns can be laid around all the exposed sides of the camp, quickly and without fatigue, and this affords great

---

[1] A defence made of felled trees with boughs pointing outwards.

security during the night and gives confidence to the tirailleurs. Complete protection is assured by pickets placed, according to the lie of the land, at 110 to 200 yards in advance of the abattis.

As it was necessary to reckon with the possible lapse of the tirailleurs—nearly all newly enrolled and apt to be overcome by sleep—patrols made frequent rounds of the pickets and sentinels. The European officers and non-commissioned officers relieved each other often during the night, to ensure the efficient surveillance of our guard.

These minute and burdensome precautions seemed indispensable, and by their means we were able to avoid all surprise. Twice, between Soumpi and Niodougou, and at Mékoré, the Touareg approached our camp to make a night attack. They were compelled to give it up because of the efficiency of our guard.

THE NATIVES

Between Diartou and Timbuctoo the population is divided into two distinct parts:

F

1. The people who live by their own labour;

2. The Touareg, with their vassals and slaves, who sweat the working people.

The working people were tired of the extortions and inroads of the Touareg, who had become more and more exacting, especially since our taking of the Macina the previous year, which showed them that our arrival was imminent and meant the end of their plundering. The working people consist of:

Peulhs, who live by their flocks, which they pasture in the vast meadows;

Bambaras and Sarakollets, agricultural labourers who harvest millet, rice and wheat;

Djennenkés, who cultivate the soil and are also engaged in commerce;

Moors who are shepherds and merchants.

The Touareg do not work. They have flocks which they leave to the care of their captives.

The inhabitants of the country paid them regularly heavy taxes. Besides, the Touareg often made raids on the villages, where they took whatever they pleased: captives, clothes, grain, flocks. They frequently boarded the working people's pirogues, carrying goods between Timbuctoo and the Macina, and took whatever they chose from the cargoes. The terrified people, not daring to resist them, let them do as they would.

In such a state of things we could only follow one line of conduct.

We must reassure the honest population, make them understand that the era of plundering was about to have an end, and that every man should enjoy the fruits of his own toil.

It was to be expected that the people should at first feel doubtful, fearing that as soon as we had passed by we should abandon them, and dreading the Targui who would show themselves more cruel than before if allowed to come back after we had gone.

But it was certain that in the end the people would confide entirely in those who ensured them security and the peaceful enjoyment of the product of their labour.

THE COMBAT OF NIAFOUNKÉ (20*th January*)

As soon as we arrived, the canton of Aoussa-Katawal placed itself under our protection. It seemed at first that Niafounké would do the same. On entering the latter province on the 19th January, we found at Tondidaro two messengers from its chief, Nioukou, who caused all necessary provisions in millet and sheep to be given us.

I had myself sent two agents to Niafounké to invite Nioukou to come and meet me at Tondidaro. I intended to have him come to Timbuctoo.

The two agents returned in the evening of the 19th, bringing with them Babakar, nephew and heir of Nioukou, with a message from Nioukou that he would subscribe to all that his nephew might say.

The two agents, however, seemed to show some reserve ; and, after a long interrogatory, which lasted well into the night, they ended by saying that Nioukou's people had insulted them and even menaced them with arms.[1]

[1] I learned afterwards that this change of attitude of the Niafounké people was due to their receiving news of the

As such actions must be punished, it was decided to march on Niafounké.

This city, being near the Niger, was surrounded by the inundations, and these had formed three small marigots (lakes made by overflowing rivers) which must be crossed in order to reach the city. One of these marigots, the nearest to Niafounké, was 2 km. wide and in some parts 1·20 metres deep.

The troops left Tondidaro on the 20th January, at 5.30 in the morning. A flying column, under the direct orders of the commandant, comprised the 10th Company of Soudanese Tirailleurs under Captain Cristofari, one section of mountain guns of 80 mm., and 1 platoon of the squadron of Soudanese Spahis.[1] This column marched on Niafounké, followed immediately by the remainder of the column which halted and camped before the first marigot, under the orders of Captain Prost.

combat of the 15th January, in which the colonel and his staff had been killed.

[1] Corps of native cavalry in Africa: There are four regiments. The staffs are half French and half native up to and including the rank of lieutenant. (Translator.)

The horses tried in vain to cross the first marigot, which was the least difficult, but they sank in the mud, and we were compelled to leave them and our artillery at Captain Prost's camp.

Meanwhile the company of infantry continued the march. By 11.25 they had crossed the third and last marigot, and at 11.50 we were before Niafounké 890 yards away, and from the plateau where we were we could observe perfectly well the town and its approaches.

The warriors, to the number of about 400, stood in line before the town, while their griots chanted battle songs to excite them.

The first platoon was at the front and opened fire, the second standing in reserve. The instant our first volley was fired the Niafounké warriors rushed forward to the attack. A group of their cavalry advanced at a gallop and tried to flank our right. Lieutenant Frèrejean wheeled his section to the right, moved rapidly to the top of a ridge from which he had a good aim at the enemy's cavalry, and stopped them short with his volleys.

The attack on our front, though extremely vigorous, was also checked by the volleys of the first platoon. A number of the enemy were killed within 25 metres of our lines. In less than a quarter of an hour the enemy was in flight, leaving a hundred dead on the field. Pursuit was impossible as our cavalry had not been able to come with us. Nioukou, though wounded in the arm, succeeded in making his escape.

Two of our sections then searched the houses, which had been abandoned by all the able-bodied men. They brought together a large number of women and children who had not had time to fly from the other side of the river for lack of pirogues, and these were assembled outside the village. There it was explained to them that we had come to punish their warriors for the insults they had offered us, and that we should not in any way molest the weak and defenceless.[1]

[1] We learned afterwards that Nioukou, who had taken refuge at Arabébé, had wanted the women and their children to come there; but the women had refused to go, saying that, contrary to the custom among the blacks, we had done them no harm. The inhabitants consequently returned to Niafounké, and the depopulation of this rich country was avoided.

The column therefore left them at Nia-founké, starting at 4.15 in the afternoon and reaching Captain Prost's camp at 6 o'clock. We had no losses in this affair.

The March on Mékoré and Atta

Some native shepherds whom we met on the road were sent to Ali-Habana, chief of the canton of Atta, to invite him to come to Mékoré to meet the commandant of the column. The village of Mékoré is near the road that goes to Goundam. The visit of Ali-Habana would enable us to adjust various matters which were then awaiting settlement, and at the same time would not much retard our march on Goundam.

On the 24th January, Captain Pouy-debat, with a platoon of infantry and the auxiliary Spahis, was left under the guard of the convoy near the camp where we had passed the night beside the Lake of Fati. The rest of the column started for Mékoré 7 miles further on the same lake.

We had hardly started when two messengers brought a letter from their chief in which he promised to meet us at Mékoré. At the same time he asked how much grain and how many sheep we needed, so that he could have these taken to Mékoré.

The messengers explained that Ali-Habana was very old, that it was difficult for him to go about, and asked if his son might not come in his stead.

Two of our messengers then went away with the others to carry our reply, in which I insisted that Ali-Habana should come himself, but at the same time agreed to the substitution of his son if that should be impossible.

We arrived at 8.15 at the village of Mékoré, which we found almost entirely abandoned. At noon new messengers from Ali-Habana brought us presents from their chief, with his compliments. They thought that he was coming, but when they had left Atta he had not yet received our emissaries.

At 2 p.m. nothing had arrived, and the column began its march on Atta. We had gone but a short distance when our messengers returned, saying that Ali-

Habana was coming to Mékoré with everything that had been asked of him. A
number of his people accompanied our
emissaries.

Our agents, whose devotion and loyalty I
have many times had occasion to appreciate,
declared that Ali-Habana would come to
Mékoré, but could not reach there before 6
o'clock, as on account of his advanced age
he was obliged to travel in a pirogue, and
that our march on Atta would terrify the
natives. The column was therefore ordered
to return to camp at Mékoré.

At midnight Ali-Habana had not yet
come, and we were informed that his people
who had come to Mékoré to gather
the provisions, had fled. It was then
decided to march on Atta.

The squadron of Spahis started at 2.45 in
the morning of the 25th January, left the
platoon of du Laurens at Korango, and
arrived at Atta at 6 o'clock. The infantry
and artillery left Mékoré at 4.50 and halted
off Korango at 8 o'clock in the morning,
advices sent by Captain Prost informing
them that the squadron was strong enough

to accomplish its mission at Atta. All the villages were abandoned by the inhabitants, but we found in them a considerable quantity of grain, and were able to re-victual the convoy which was then completely out of provisions. Unfortunately we could not get any pirogues, which might be needed to cross the marigot of Goundam. The natives had taken all their pirogues with them, transporting everything they could carry away to the islets in the midst of the floods of the Niger, and there we could not reach them as we had no boats.

The squadron of Spahis returned at 7 in the evening to camp at Mékoré, where it passed the night, it being too late to proceed any further.

The rest of the column reached Pouyde-bat's camp at 6.15 in the evening.

THE MARCH ON GOUNDAM

The platoon of tirailleurs under Lieutenant Maillac and the auxiliary Spahis, who had not marched for two days, started at midnight for Goundam under the command of

Captain Pouydebat, to capture by surprise the pirogues used in crossing the marigot at that place. They arrived at 5.30 in the morning on the left bank of the marigot, at a point opposite the city.

But they found the Touareg assembled on the other bank, and surrounding the city. Their pirogues had been destroyed. The marigot in its narrowest part was 330 yards wide, and the current was very rapid. The best swimmers went into the water to ascertain whether the marigot could not be crossed by a group consisting of all the men able to swim, and important enough to secure a point on the opposite bank. But they were carried away by the current and compelled to hurry back to shore, having been able to cross only a narrow strip of water.

The main body of our troops rejoined the Pouydebat detachment on the 26th January, at 4 o'clock in the afternoon, and the squadron of Spahis arrived the next day at 8 in the morning.

The reconnaissances which had been made in the surrounding country and the information thus obtained proved beyond doubt the impossibility of finding any other crossing.

It was necessary to cross the marigot at Goundam, and for that purpose to procure pirogues.

THE TENDIRMA EXPEDITION

A light column composed of the squadron of Spahis and the Puypéroux half-company was placed under the command of Captain Prost.

It started on the 27th, at 6 o'clock in the evening, with orders to go to Tendirma by the road which skirts the eastern side of the mountain of Fati, so as to avoid the villages situated on the lake of that name. Tendirma being at some distance from the place where the column was at that time, there was a chance that the inhabitants, or at least some of them, were still there with their pirogues.

The Prost detachment arrived at Tendirma at 4 o'clock in the morning, after an all-night march. The village was practically empty. They found, however, three pirogues in good condition and some somonos to propel them.

The inhabitants of Tendirma and of the other villages in the canton of Atta had taken refuge on an island about 780 yards from Tendirma. There they had taken a quantity of grain and some sheep. The three captured pirogues were got ready, and Captain Puypéroux, Lieutenant Robillot and about 20 tirailleurs and Spahis got into pirogues at midday and made for the island. They were received with shots, and replied with several volleys which killed 25 or 30 of the enemy. The latter scattered and fled as soon as we landed. On our side one tirailleur was wounded by a bullet.

The Puypéroux half-company landed and went to work to collect the grain necessary for provisioning the column. A fourth pirogue was seized, and the morning of the 29th was passed in transporting to Tendirma the provisions found the day before in the island.

The entire Prost detachment, bringing

these provisions and 750 sheep and goats, arrived in the evening of the 30th at the head of the lake of Fati, where the pirogues were also brought.

On the 31st this detachment started for Goundam, followed by the four pirogues borne by 200 porters, who arrived at 5 o'clock in the evening at the camp of the column.

CROSSING THE MARIGOT OF GOUNDAM

At-the sight of the pirogues the Touareg became much excited, and a loud clamour could be heard in their camps. They moved in a body to the isthmus of a peninsula opposite our camp, where we must embark to cross the river. Our two mountain guns of 80 mm., and a platoon of infantry drawn up on our shore opened fire on the Touareg, who lost several men and immediately scattered. All night they continued their flight to the north, carrying with them all they could take, and robbing the inhabitants of Goundam of nearly all their provisions. On the morning of the 1st

February, when we started to cross the marigot the last Touareg left Goundam.

As the four pirogues had been slightly injured in their transportation by land, they were now repaired.

They were launched at 8 o'clock in the morning of 1st February, and the passage of the marigot began at once. We were compelled to stop at 8 in the evening, as the strong current made the crossing dangerous during the night, which was very dark. At this time the Cristofari company, a platoon of Spahis, and the staff were on the other bank.

A letter from Captain Philippe, received at 11 o'clock in the morning, informed us of the arrival at Goundam of the flotilla,[1] with one company and a half of tirailleurs and one section of mountain guns of 80 mm. It also gave us the painful news of the combat of "Tacoubâo" on the 15th January.

To hasten its arrival, Naval Lieutenant

---

[1] This was the flotilla which had carried Colonel Bonnier's column (*vide* Introduction), and was coming back from Timbuctoo.

Boiteux had kept his flotilla in motion day and night. It reached Goundam on 2nd February at 2.30 in the morning. The two barges and the pirogues which he had brought facilitated our crossing of the marigot, and we were on the other side by noon of 3rd February. The troops commanded by Captain Philippe had arrived on 2nd February at nightfall.

THE MARCH ON FARASCH

A marching column was now organised, consisting of two companies and a half of tirailleurs, two sections of mountain guns of 80 mm. and the squadron of Spahis. The convoy, along with a platoon of tirailleurs, the auxiliary Spahis, and the flotilla, were left at Goundam.

On the 4th the column started for Farasch, 31 miles to the north, where the Touareg had taken refuge.

The column camped in the evening at Karao-Kamba, after having marched over a very rough and difficult country. The Touareg, however, on hearing the news of

G

our departure, left Farasch for Oum-el-
Djérane, four stages to the north-east. The
roads were very bad; the porters, exhausted
by the long and rapid march from Ségou to
Goundam, kept up with the greatest difficulty; some of them fell down and could
not get up again. Furthermore, our provisions were nearly gone, and we had no
chance of renewing them until we reached
Timbuctoo. Even if we should get to Oum-
el-Djérane, the Touareg would not wait for
us there, but would continue their flight to
the north, constantly gaining on us.

Therefore orders were given for the return
to Goundam, where we arrived on 6th
February in the morning.

The Value of having a Post at Goundam

The inhabitants of this city had submitted
on 1st February, immediately after the departure of the Touareg. Closely watched
by the latter, it had not been possible for
them to join with us sooner. They hoped
that our arrival would prove to be their

deliverance; that they would no longer be compelled to suffer the pillage, violence, and even murders of which they had continually been the victims. They earnestly begged us to establish a post at Goundam for their protection.

The strategical position of Goundam is very important, as it is the only point where the marigot can be crossed. Commanding this position, we could prevent the Touareg from entering the fertile villages of the Killi and of the Kissou, where they got their supplies of grain, and from keeping their flocks near the inundations of the Niger, where they are constantly pastured. Finally, it would be easy to watch over the rich cantons of Atta and Niafounké, which we would prohibit the Touareg from entering, thus shutting them off from all access to the river and putting a stop to their piratical attacks on the traders' pirogues.

Unfortunately, we now had no more provisions, and from Goundam, which had been pillaged by the Touareg, only a few days' rations were to be obtained. Under these circumstances, we could only establish

a post at Goundam on condition that it
would be provisioned immediately after our
arrival at Timbuctoo. But, on the other
hand, I had learned from Captain Philippe
that at Timbuctoo I should find despatches
recalling me to Kayes, transferring the command to the senior captain, limiting us
to the occupation of Timbuctoo and the
establishment of police patrols around the
city, and even suggesting the possibility of
an evacuation.

In this uncertainty I did not see my way
to order the establishment of a post at
Goundam which some day might have to
be evacuated with great danger to the
inhabitants of reprisals on the part of the
Touareg. Furthermore, the Touareg were
now far away in the north, in great fear of
our troops, and it would always be easy,
if the instructions of the government per-
mitted, to return later to Goundam.

From Goundam to Timbuctoo

On 7th February the column started by
land for Timbuctoo, skirting the inundations. The convoy went down the marigot

in pirogues, escorted by the flotilla which was reinforced by a platoon of tirailleurs.

At 8 in the evening we arrived near Tacoubâo, the scene of the combat of 15th January. The morning of the 9th was devoted to the identification of the bodies which we found there.

Eleven European officers and two non-commissioned officers had been killed, and their bodies were all found.

We also found the bodies of 64 natives, which we buried on the spot.

The bodies of the Europeans were brought together and taken to Timbuctoo for burial.

We at length reached Timbuctoo on 12th February at one o'clock, the flotilla and the convoy having been there since the 10th.

During the long march from Ségou to Timbuctoo, the column lost two tirailleurs, who died of illness, and had one tirailleur wounded who afterwards recovered.

We had covered a distance of 508 miles, including the 48 miles of the marches on Niafounké, Atta and Karao-Kamba.

CHAPTER II

OCCUPATION OF THE REGION

THE troops were now in urgent need of rest. It was necessary to drill and manœuvre them again for some time as they were composed of young soldiers, raw and unfinished, and it was necessary to take them again in hand.

Besides, we were in an entirely unknown country, about which we had to obtain accurate information. The Touareg tribes had fled before our troops, leaving us a free passage and placing themselves beyond our reach. By our entry into Timbuctoo we had taken undisputed possession of the country. It was now necessary to give the tribes, which had been neutral until now, time to send in their submission. It was also necessary to allow the Touareg tribes which had fought us, time to become disorganised in the barren country where they had taken refuge, and where, owing to our lack of transportation facilities, we could not pursue them. This disorganisation would soon be complete, however, if we prevented them from entering the fertile countries of the Killi and the Kissou, between Timbuctoo and Goundam, which belonged to them and upon which they subsisted.

The first thing to be done was to quarter our troops at Timbuctoo. On our arrival there I had found all the despatches addressed to the commandant supérieur and Major Hugueny. I was ordered to return to Kayes to resume the superintendence of the railroad. But when these instructions were sent the news of the combat of the 15th January and its sad results had not been received. I considered that under such circumstances my duty was to stay, and as senior officer I took command of all the troops and of the flotilla. This point of view was confirmed by the governor who, in his despatch No. 251 of 13th February, placed me in command of Timbuctoo.

FORT BONNIER

It was important that the troops should be lodged as comfortably as possible in their barracks, so as to be able to recover from the fatigues they must inevitably undergo in every expedition they would have to make.

A fort, of which the plan is shown in the sketch herewith, was begun a few days after our arrival with such workmen and materials as Timbuctoo and all the villages of the Kissou could furnish. This fort was large enough to accommodate all the troops, and two sections sufficed to guard it, each being stationed in one of the blockhouses which protected its flanks. Situated south of the city near the landing place, it commanded the communication with the river, and also commanded the city, from which it was separated by a protecting zone of 55 yards. Captain Aurenche, of the naval artillery, was given charge of the work, which he pushed with great activity. At the time of writing, the enclosing earth-works, 10 feet high,

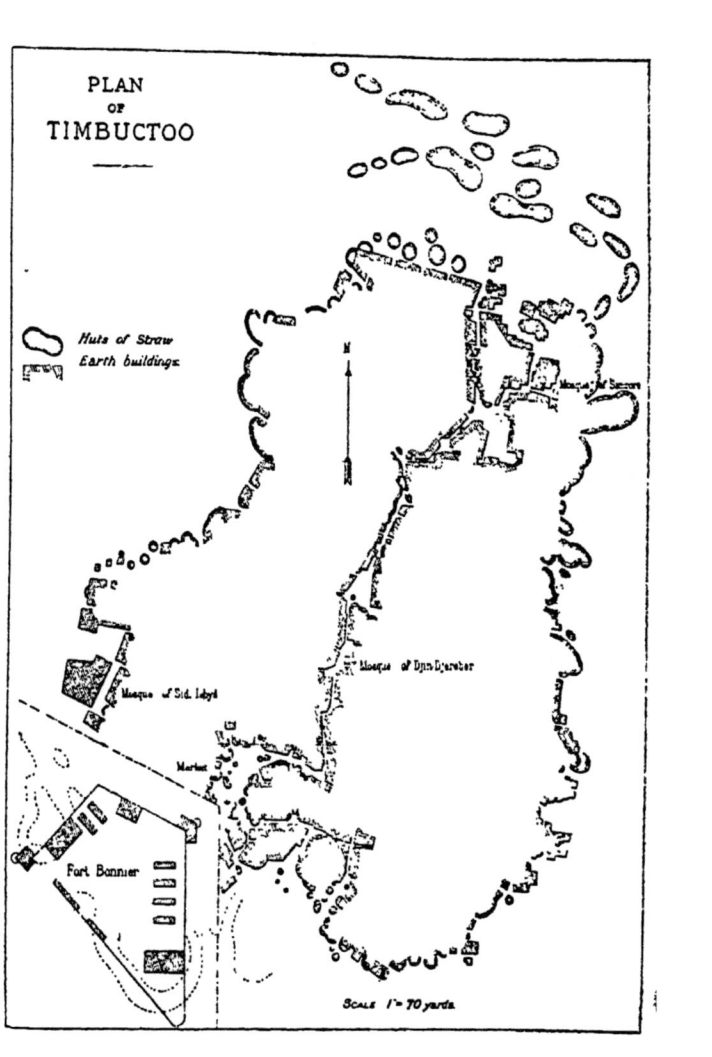

PLAN
OF
TIMBUCTOO

Huts of Straw
Earth buildings.

M

Mosque of Sidi Jahya

Mosque of Djin Djareber

Market

Fort Bonnier

SCALE 1"= 70 yards.

and the flanking cupolas are finished. A vast storehouse, holding 600 tons, lodgings for all the Europeans, and provisional shelters for natives, have been built or arranged in the interior of the fort.

This work was given the name of Fort Bonnier, in honour of the heroic victim of the combat of 15th January.

THE KABARA BLOCKHOUSE

A marigot, starting from Koriumé and passing by Kabara, affords passage for pirogues from the river to the port of Timbuctoo. Up to the time of our coming the flotilla had remained at Kabara, and communication between Timbuctoo and the river was thus ensured. In order to avoid losing entirely the use of our boats a blockhouse was built at Kabara by workmen from Timbuctoo. This work, conducted by Captain Cristofari, is, at the time of writing, finished, 30 men being sufficient for its defence.

This first blockhouse soon became inadequate. In fact, by the 15th April, the

pirogues could no longer go as far as Timbuctoo, and Kabara became the port of
arrival and departure of all the convoys.
On account of the excellent quality of
fodder, and the extensive pasturage here, it
was made the base for our cavalry and
flocks.

It was therefore necessary to extend and
supplement our works. Captain Jacques
was ordered to organise: 1st, a flotilla of
pirogues brought to us by the different
villages in that region; 2nd, a repair shop
for these pirogues; 3rd, a clearing-house;
4th, sheep-folds, a camp for the Spahis, and
one for the auxiliary drivers and the animals
not in use at Timbuctoo. All these annexes
were surrounded by thorny hedges, which
protected them from sudden attacks.

For a month past the pirogues had no
longer been able to reach Kabara, and had
to stop at Daye, 2 miles lower than this
post. There they were guarded by a section
of infantry. As for a period of two months
or two months and a half, beginning about
15th July, navigation would have to stop
at Koriumé, 4 miles from Kabara, a

defensive post was built near Koriumé, at
Adjitafé, where it was intended that our
pirogues and convoys should lie in harbour.
The barges of the flotilla, provided with
machine guns, were to stay at this post.
They were to assist the post in protecting
our pirogues, and, moreover, they would
prevent the Touareg on the right bank from
making inroads on the left.

The Occupation of Goundam

It was indispensable to have a post at
Goundam in order to check the entrance
of the Touareg into the Killi and the
Kissou, and to prevent them from bringing
their flocks on to the land along the inundations, and practising their piracy on the
river.

The instructions of the governor then
allowing more liberty of action than at the
beginning, and the government having
announced its intention to keep Timbuctoo
and to send reinforcements for this purpose,
the occupation of Goundam was decided.
As the inhabitants of Dongoï had already

notified us of the appearance of bands of Touareg along the inundations, looking for pirogues to take them to the villages of the Kissou, the 9th company, under Captain Pansier, had been sent to reconnoitre the marigot of Goundam. Leaving in pirogues, on 20th February, this detachment had visited the villages of Tassakant, Douékiré, Dongoï and Galaga, and had returned on the 26th to Timbuctoo. The Touareg, warned by their sentinels, had evacuated the shores.

A column composed of the 11th company of tirailleurs under Captain Philippe, the Maillac platoon of the 10th company, three platoons of the squadron of Spahis, and one section of mountain guns of 80 mm., started from Timbuctoo on 5th March, under the command of Captain Prost. When they reached Goundam on 8th March at four o'clock in the afternoon, after a four days' march, they found the Touareg in the act of crossing the marigot. Cannon and rifles were fired at the enemy on the water and on the other bank. The cavalry charged on the remainder, some of whom tried to save themselves by swimming, and others were killed. A flock of 1000 sheep was captured.

The column camped close to the town. The Fort of Goundam was planned and its construction begun with the help of workmen from the town. The Maillac platoon returned to Timbuctoo in pirogues with the Sadioka section, which had escorted to Goundam the convoy bringing one month's rations to the post.

The building of the fort had been begun under the direction of Captain Fourgeot, but owing to the limited resources of the country, entirely pillaged by the Touareg, the work could not be pushed as rapidly as at Timbuctoo. Nevertheless, the store was completed, and the lodgings for the Europeans would soon be ready for use. These new constructions, with the houses already occupied in the village, formed a whole which was well organised for defence and beyond danger from any attack.

CHAPTER III

THE GEOGRAPHY OF THE REGION

ONE of our chief pre-occupations, after reaching Timbuctoo, had been to understand the country and its inhabitants as soon as possible, in order to discover the best policy for pacifying it and utilising its resources. We also wanted to turn to account every means it could offer in our work of suppressing the hostile tribes. At first the native villagers were not willing to tell us what they knew. But their confidence in us increased little by little when they saw, by our work at Timbuctoo and Goundam, that it was our fixed purpose to remain in the country, and were convinced of our undeniable superiority by our defeat of the resisting Touareg. However, we were compelled to wait several months before they would give us the information we wanted.

The region of Timbuctoo—that is to say, the country which for a long time had shared the changing fortunes of this city, and was under the sway of the Touareg, masters of Timbuctoo—comprised, besides the city, the following :

The Aoussa-Katawal, the Soboundou-Samba, the Tioki, the Killi, the Kissou, the Fitouka, the Gourma, and the Azaouad.

THE CITY OF TIMBUCTOO

Population.—The population of Timbuctoo, which may be roughly estimated as 7000 or 8000, is not homogeneous, but composed of the most varied elements. It is formed chiefly of two distinct races; the Rouma, descendants of the ancient Moroccan conquerors, and the Hératine, descendants of the black Songhays, subjected by the Rouma. Another small group known as the Tolba consists of people who came from all parts of the Soudan to study Arabic at Timbuctoo, and who have been settled in this city for a very long time.

A few Toucouleurs, Songhays, Bambaras

(who are almost all slaves), nomad Arabs, people of the Tafilalet and the Touat, Moroccans and Tripolitans complete the population.

Besides this permanent population there is always a large number of transient visitors who come from every part of the Sahara and the Soudan.

Commerce.—The commercial importance of Timbuctoo, which has greatly diminished since the Touareg became absolute masters of the country, that is, for nearly a century, is due to its geographical position.

Situated, for all practical purposes, on the Niger (for, thanks to the inundations of this river which extend far northward, the largest native pirogues, carrying as much as 100 tons of merchandise, can come as far as the walls of the city in the rainy season), and lying nearest to such Saharan countries as can trade with the Soudan, it became naturally the dépôt of exchange for goods coming from those parts.

Furthermore, placed as it is below the numerous tributaries and branches of the Niger, by which the products of the Soudan come in, it is necessarily the point where all these products converge.

Timbuctoo has therefore become a great market, or rather a great warehouse where the products of the north and south are interchanged; but its commercial importance has been considerably increased by the proximity of the Taodenni mines, which supply the populations of the Niger loop with all their salt.

Of itself the city produces nothing; its inhabitants live almost exclusively by trade. A few are engaged in the manufacture of woollen and cotton blankets and of embroidered garments, which they sell in the north and in the Touareg country.

The principal countries which carry on a regular commerce with Timbuctoo, are— in the Sahara region—South Morocco, the region of Tindouf occupied by the Tadjakant nomads, the Touat and the Tafilalet.

The imports of these countries consist chiefly of stuffs of European manufacture, principally from England, of sugar, tea, spices, glass beads, arms, and copper and iron articles. All these goods come from Souira

H

in Morocco; they are bought by the nomad Arabs either at this port or at the market of Souk-Sidi-Ahmed or Moussa which is in South Morocco, and is supplied with these goods by the Moroccan merchants. At Timbuctoo are also found tobacco and dates from the Touat and the Tafilalet, as well as tanned skins and wrought leather from Tindouf.

These goods are transported on camels, chiefly by the Tadjakant nomads, but also by those of the Touat and of the Tafilalet.

Another nomad tribe, the Bérabiche, which occupies the Azaouad between Taodenni and Timbuctoo, almost monopolises the transportation of salt, of which a large quantity is imported. Throughout the year salt-laden camels enter Timbuctoo, but it is principally at the beginning of autumn, before the winter season, and in spring that this trade is most active. During these seasons the Bérabiche combine with another nomad tribe less important than themselves, the Kounta from the region of Mabrouck and of the Adrar, to organise two long caravans of 3000 to 4000 camels each, all laden with salt.

There are two main caravan roads : that of Araouane for South Morocco and the mines of Taodenni, and that of Boudjebiha for the Touat, the Tafilalet, the region of Mabrouck and the Adrar.

The exports to these countries consist of grain, millet and rice, Karité butter, raw and woven cotton, native stuffs of the Soudan, raw hides, for the past few years a small quantity of gold and ivory, silver coins, jewels, and, lastly, slaves.

In the Soudan proper, Timbuctoo trades with all the countries watered by the river as far as Sansandig, with the Mossi by Bandiagara, the country of Kong by Djenné, the Humbori by the Gourma and, lastly, all the eastern country as far as Gogo.

The imports of these countries consist of millet, rice, ground-nuts, Karité butter, spices, cotton, raw and in strips, special stuffs of the Soudan, ostrich plumes coming chiefly from the Humbori, wrought leather, gold, ivory, pottery, etc.

The exports are principally salt, stuffs

and tobacco; there is also a limited trade in glass beads.

It is impossible at this time to state, even approximately, the value of the imports and exports; to do that, it is necessary to wait till peace and the safety of the roads permit the resumption of the usual commerce.

Duties on Merchandise.—Goods brought by land paid no fixed duties among the Touareg, but the merchants were obliged to buy their protection by giving them presents often beyond their means. Generally, each group of merchants had an understanding with an influential Targui chief, by which they gave him sometimes annually, sometimes on the arrival of each caravan, a gratuity which more or less secured his protection.

When crossing the territory occupied by the Bérabiche, fixed duties were collected by the chief of that tribe.

The merchants of the Sahel (Tadjakant) paid for 1 load of cloth, 7 bars of salt plus $\frac{1}{3}$ of a bar; or $\frac{1}{8}$ of an ounce of gold plus $\frac{1}{3}$; for other merchandise in the same proportion.

The merchants of the Touat and of the Tafilalet paid for 1 load of cloth, 4 bars of salt; for 6 loads of tobacco, 4 bars of salt.

The merchants of the other countries paid the same rates.

At the gate of Timbuctoo, also, there were no fixed duties, but the merchants made valuable presents to the chief of the city in exchange for their protection.

Merchandise transported by the river paid "the Achour" (tenth) on entering Timbuctoo, to the Touareg Irreganaten at Koura, and to Aguibou at Saraféré; and, in addition, the merchants were obliged to give presents to the Touareg river pirates.

Salt paid no duty on entering Timbuctoo. At Taodenni, the caïd of the village collected $\frac{1}{5}$ of the salt taken from the mines.

At the time of writing, and while waiting for the proper organisation of the customs, a uniform but trifling duty has been fixed for all the caravans without exception.

The basis of this duty is 1 piece of cloth valued at from 25 to 30 francs on each load of cloth valued at from 1200 to 1500 francs.

The other duties are based on the following figures :—

1 load of tobacco is valued at from 200 to 250 frances; 1 load of sugar is valued at from 900 to 1000 francs; salt pays no duty.

THE REGION OF TIMBUCTOO

Aoussa-Katawal.—This district lies southwest between the Lake of Takadji, the Issa-Ber and the Lake of Tenda. Its permanent population is composed of Peulhs, Bambaras and Touareg mixed with Peulhs, and become sedentary. The people are occupied in grain culture and extensive sheep raising. Their territory used to be occupied also by different branches of the Touareg tribe of the "Iguellad," to whom they were in fact subject, and who imposed upon them everchanging and often very burdensome taxes.

Soboundou-Samba.—Situated also southwest, between the Lake of Takadji, the Lake of Horo and the Issa-Ber, the stationary population of this country is made up almost entirely of Peulhs, who are shepherds and farmers. Like the preceding district, it also used to be overrun by Iguellad, who were its real masters.

Tioki.—This district lies also to the south-west, between the Lake of Horo, the Lake of Fati and the Issa-Ber. Peopled with Peulhs, who are shepherds and farmers, this country was under the yoke of the Iguellad and of another Touareg tribe, the Tengueriguif.

Killi.—Situated in the west, between the Lake of Fati, the western branch of the Goundam marigot and the river. This country is occupied by both nomad and stationary populations: Peuhls and Songhays who live in the villages and are nearly all farmers; Cheurfiga, a nomad tribe of the Berber race, doing a little farming, but occupied chiefly in sheep raising; and, lastly, the Touareg Tengueriguif, practically masters of all the Killi.

Kissou.—This country may be considered as the territory proper of Timbuctoo. It is here, indeed, that the inhabitants of the city employ their slaves in the grain fields, and it is here also that the real masters of Timbuctoo, the Tengueriguif, generally lived and kept the greater part of their slaves. This country lies between the river, the western branch of the marigot of Goundam and Timbuctoo. It is populated by the Songhays.

Fitouka.—This district lies to the south, on the banks of the Bara-Issa, between the marigot of Sarayamou and the arm of Bougouberou. Thickly populated and very fertile, this country does not seem to have been entirely subject to the Touareg. Its population consists mainly of Peulhs engaged in grain culture and some sheep raising.

Gourma or Aribinda.[1]—It is bounded on the north by the river, on the west by the marigot of Sarayamou and its prolongation towards Kaniouma, and on the south by the Humbori. Westwards it has no well-defined boundary.

Nearly barren in its eastern part, it is fertile enough in the centre in the region of Haribougo, where many pools which disappear in the dry season form excellent arable land. All along the marigot of Sarayamou, the country is thickly populated

[1] The two words, Gourma in Songhay and Aribinda in Arabian, have the same meaning, *i.e.* country situated on the right bank of the river.

by Peulhs farmers. It is overrun by the Kounta, a nomad tribe of Arab origin whose many captives work in the fields of Haribougo, and by the Touareg tribe of the Irreganaten, who, as usual, were settled along the river and pillaged the pirogues going to and coming from Timbuctoo.

Azaouad.—By this name is meant the vast region extending between the salt mines of Taodenni to the north, Mabrouck to the east, Timbuctoo to the south and El-Akla to the west. It is absolutely barren country, overrun by the Bérabiche, and traversed from north to south by the Araouane road by which all the caravans travel to Timbuctoo.

At the east and north-east of this road stretches another region called Hessiane (the wells), which is overrun by the Ahl-Sidi-Ali, the Kel-Nekounder and the Kounta.

CHAPTER IV

ETHNOGRAPHY

THE nomad tribes which live in the Timbuctoo region, or who merely have commercial relations with that city, are divided into two distinct parts : the Touareg tribes and the Arab tribes.

THE TOUAREG TRIBES

For more than a century the immediate environs of Timbuctoo, and all the region lying along the banks of the Niger between the eastern extremity of the Adrar mountains to the north-east, Gogo to the south-east, Safay to the south-west, and Ras-el-Mâ to the north-west, were dominated by the six Touareg tribes, which occupied this immense territory. These tribes were known as the Iguellad, the Tengueriguif, the Irreganaten, the Kel-Temoulaï, the

Igouadaren, and the Aouellimiden. The first four, settled near Timbuctoo, exercised a direct influence on the city, and commanded the roads which led to it; the other two tribes were not closely connected with the city.

Before studying each tribe individually, let us outline their general organisation, and the ties which bound them to one another.

Like all Touareg tribes, they comprised three distinct castes :

The "Touareg" of pure blood, composing the warrior nobility ;

The "Imghad," or vassals ;

The "Billat," or slaves.

Each noble family has sovereignty over a certain number of Imghad, whom they often subject to very hard servitude. In time of peace the Imghad are engaged in breeding and selling sheep ; in time of war they must march, willingly or otherwise, with their masters.

As to the Billat, they are usually slaves, born among the Touareg, and, consequently, very loyal to their masters, whom they always accompany to war.

The Iguellad, Tengueriguif, Irreganaten, and Kel-Temoulaï have always been connected. The first have preserved a religious influence over the rest, while the three other groups descend from a common ancestor, and bear the generic name of Tademekket. They have therefore always been allies, but the Tengueriguif, more warlike than all the others, have been the chief centre, so to speak, of this federation.

The Aouellimiden and Igouadaren (the latter being a separate branch of the former) have lived for a long time far beyond the zone of influence of the Tademekket; yet, owing to their power, they have always retained some power over the Tademekket, who pay them annual tribute.

We shall now study each of these tribes individually:

1. *Iguellad.*—The Iguellad occupy the region included between Rasel-Mâ to the west, Soumpi to the south, and Goundam to the east; they even spread beyond Timbuctoo towards the north-east, into the district of Tagane.

This tribe, as already said, has a certain

religious influence over the other Touareg.
It comprises a great many subdivisions.
Many of these, composed chiefly of marabouts, do not fight, and live apart. The
warriors, those who live more particularly
by pillage, are called Kel-Antassar. They
live in the region of Faraschoum-el-Djérane,
Ras-el-Mâ. At the time of writing, the
chief of the Kel-Antassar is Ngouna.

This tribe is generally considered poor.
It is true that they own some fine flocks of
goats and sheep, but they have few slaves
and Imghad. Besides their itinerant camps,
they own the three villages of N'bouna,
Toukabongo, and Bitagongo, situated on
the high ground bordering the marigot of
Goundam. It is in these villages and at
Ras-el-Mâ, that the slaves and the Imghad
do a little farming, and the Iguellad store
their provisions.

Travel by pirogues is possible practically
all the year round in this region.

Though they are rather numerous, the
Iguellad cannot furnish many fighting men.
Having scarcely any horses, they ride
chiefly on camels. The fighting force

of the entire tribe would aggregate about 800. They are all armed with lances, sabres, and daggers, and have very few guns.

Tengueriguif.—The Tengueriguif, more warlike and worse pillagers than all the others, used to live in the immediate environs of Timbuctoo, and were absolute masters of the city. They occupied also the country of the Killi and of the Kissou, and especially the banks of the marigot of Goundam. This village was their chief centre. Owing to their strength and their warlike spirit their influence throughout the country was very powerful, and they were able to retain numerous vassals, including the entire tribe of the Imededghen, of Berber origin, who occupied the land comprised between Timbuctoo, Goundam, and the pass of Karao-Kamba, and formed a group of 150 to 200 tents.

The possession of many flocks compelled the Tengueriguif to stay near the water. Therefore, during the flood season, they camped along the inundations between Goundam and Timbuctoo, and in the dry season on the banks of the Niger, in the Killi and the Kissou.

Living in tents and possessing hardly any camels, the Tengueriguif are compelled to use dépôts where they stow away the grain harvested by their slaves or brought in as tithes by the villages of the Kissou and the Killi, which they mercilessly fleece. They also store in the same places all the impedimenta which might increase the difficulty of their frequent journeys from one camp to another.

These dépôts all lie in the Goundam marigot valley, where the Tengueriguif employ their slaves in the grain fields.

During the greater part of the year this region can be reached in pirogues, although small pirogues only can be used in the dry season.

The present chief of the Tengueriguif is Mohammed-Oueld-Ouab. The tribe is subdivided into six parts, furnishing altogether 700 warriors, 130 of whom are horsemen armed with lances, sabres, and daggers. They have no rifles.

In time of war they can always rely on

the support of their neighbours, the Iguellad, and of their kindred the Irreganaten and Kel-Temoulaï.

Irreganaten.—The Irreganaten occupy the right bank of the river in the region of the Island of Koura, spreading southward into the Gourma which forms the eastern boundary of the new States of the Macina and extends as far as Humbori.

Their authority reaches to the Binga, a district lying between the river and the marigot of Sarayamou north of the Fitouka.

The Irreganaten are settled chiefly on the shores of the river in the region of the Island of Koura; and from these parts they make their pillaging attacks upon the pirogues going to or returning from Timbuctoo. Their influence is undoubtedly felt in all the villages of this region.

At the time of writing their chief was Assalmi, but he did not wield an equal sway over all the subdivisions of the tribe. Some of them work independently on the river, and do not always acknowledge the authority of this chief. Their wealth is mainly in their herds of cattle, goats, and sheep.

The power of the Irreganaten is about
equal to that of the Tengueriguif; and
they can therefore furnish 180 horsemen
and 400 foot soldiers. Their inferiority to
the Tengueriguif in the number of infantry
is due to their having fewer Imghad and
slaves.

Kel-Temoulaï.—The Kel-Temoulaï used
to inhabit the region comprised between
Kabara on the west and Bani on the east.
At the time of writing they are settled
chiefly on the right bank of the river, but
none the less continue their pillaging on the
left bank. All the villages on the shores
of the river lying between the two points
mentioned above are subject to them.

Their present chief is Aberdi, and though
he lives on the left bank, he is ruler also of
the Kel-Temoulaï on the right bank.

The Kel-Temoulaï are regarded as better
pillagers than warriors, and are much less
numerous than the other Tademekket.
They can furnish from 70 to 80 horsemen
and 200 foot soldiers, armed with sabres,
lances, and daggers.

Igouadaren.—The Igouadaren occupy

I

both sides of the river from Immelal on the west to Aguadech on the east. They are divided into two groups—the Igoua-daren-Aouza (the word "Aouza" means, in this country, everything situated on the left bank of the river), and the Igouadaren-Aribinda on the right bank. At certain times these two sub-tribes unite; at others, separated by renewed dissensions, they return to their separate camps.

Ordinarily they have two chiefs, but at the present time they are all under the rule of Sekhaoui, chief of the Igouadaren-Aouza.

The territory of the Igouadaren-Aouza is bounded on the north by a line passing at about a two or three days' march from the river; on the east, by the village of Aguadech; on the south by the river (except in the rainy season, when they go into the Aribinda to pasture their flocks); and on the west by the village of Immelal. All the villages or camps lying between those two places are subject to them.

The Igouadaren-Aribinda inhabit nearly all the region known as Aribinda; they possess a few villages on the right bank of the Niger, and spread as far as the district of Haribongo on the west and Humbori on the south.

The combined Igouadaren are very numerous—they can furnish 350 horsemen and 2000 foot soldiers, all armed with lances, sabres, and daggers. But to obtain this relatively important result, the whole of the two sub-tribes must unite.

We said in the beginning that the Igouadaren had but slight relations with the region of Timbuctoo ; they still exert, however, a certain influence over the Tademekket.

They themselves stand in great fear of the Aouellimiden, and annually pay a sort of tribute to the chief of this powerful tribe.

According to all our information it would not be to the advantage of the Igouadaren to support the Tademekket in the Timbuctoo region. Their own country is very rich, yielding them large rice harvests and excellent pasturage for their numerous flocks. There is every reason, therefore, why they should remain quietly in their homes.

Aouellimiden.—The Aouellimiden are the most powerful tribe of all the Touareg whom we have under consideration. They occupy the country which lies between the eastern extremity of the Adrar mountains to the east, Es-Pouk to the north, Mabrouck, El-Hille and Tosaye to the west, and Gogo to the south.

Their distance from Timbuctoo where they go but seldom (it used to be to collect taxes levied on the Tademekket and on the city) has prevented our getting reliable information as to their strength. Furthermore, it seems nearly certain that we shall not have any trouble with them in the Timbuctoo region.

They have always been considered as very numerous and very powerful.

NOTES ON THE TOUAREG

If we consider in general the manner of living of the Touareg, we shall see at once that their existence is dependent upon a great many conditions.

Their greatest wealth consists in flocks,

and to ensure them adequate pasturage they must be ready for constant changes of base, and consequently must live in tents, separated into small groups. Moreover, they must always stay in the neighbourhood of water.

Again, this nomadic life prevents their carrying with them any great quantity of provisions, which would encumber them.

If then, for any reason, one of their tribes is compelled to assemble at a given point, the reunion can only last a few days on account of lack of sufficient pasturage for their flocks and food for themselves. This explains why the number of Touareg is out of all proportion to the immense spaces they occupy.

These observations apply not only to one complete tribe, that is, to the reunion of all the families and all the flocks of the same group, but also to the warriors or pillagers who might wish to gather in great numbers.

Given the independent character of the Touareg, there would first be dissensions, inevitable in an assembly where numerous chiefs desired exclusive command, and afterwards a lack of provisions which would promptly compel them to disperse ; because not even the products of their pillage would enable them to live long together. And if they lived among the other tribes the result would only be mutual pillage—which has already occurred among the Tengueriguif and the Iguellad.

A coalition of all the Touareg is therefore not to be feared.

It is proper to consider, with these tribes, a few small groups of nomads of Berber origin. These are :

The Ahl-Sidi-Ali. — They occupy the region of Hessiane in the east. These Berber nomads, descendants of the Iguellad, are completely separate from them. Essentially religious in nature, they are not in the least warlike, and live peacefully on the products of their flocks. Their number can be estimated at about 100 tents.

The Kel-Nekounder.—In the country of Tagane to the east, they form a group of religious nomads, also of Iguellad origin but living by themselves. Their number can be estimated at about 50 tents. They are peaceful shepherds.

The Kel-es-Souk. — These peaceful religious people live on the shores of the river to the east, between Iloua and Immelal, forming a group of about 50 tents.

The Kel-Incheria.—Originally Iguellad, they live apart from them, with the Ahl-Sidi-Ali, comprising about 50 tents.

The Cheurfiga.—This is a nomad tribe of Berber origin, living in the Touareg manner and forming a group of about 200 tents. They inhabit the Killi, and submit absolutely to the authority of the Tengueriguif. They are rather religious shepherds and farmers than warriors.

The Ahl-Aouza.—They were originally Iguellad, but for a very long period have lived entirely separate from that tribe. Formerly they were faithful servants to the family of the sheik Sidi-Bakay, of the Kounta tribe, at the period when this family dominated the country. But later, when it lost influence, the Ahl-Aouza came under the rule of the Tengueriguif.

They are peaceful and religious, asking

only to be let alone. Essentially nomad and occupied in sheep-raising, they form a group of about 150 tents. They are settled between Dongoï and Bourem. Their chief is Saïd-ben-Faki.

Chioukh.—The Chioukh are religious Berbers who have long lived with the Irreganaten. The latter regard them as their protégés, and pay them the contributions which Mussulmans give to their religious.

They seem to have occupied the region of Haribongo for a very long period, and are considered the true proprietors of this country. The Kounta pay them the Lekkat tax (tax on agriculture) for permission to cultivate the fields.

The Chioukh are a very small tribe, having only 10 tents. But they rule over 225 tents of vassals, who are mainly farmers. They have but few flocks.

The country over which they wander lies between Haribongo, Sarayamou, and Sankaré, near Bounambougou. They have only one village, Oréséno, consisting of straw huts, and situated 10 km. east of Sarayamou.

Their chief is Lanoune-ben-Mouak.

ARAB TRIBES

The principal tribes of Arab nomads are the " Bérabiche " and the " Kounta."

Bérabiche. — Their territory, generally known by the name of Azaouad, lies between the Taodenni salt mines to the north, Mabrouck to the east, Timbuctoo to the south, and El-Akéla to the west.

This is essentially a nomad tribe, whose chief wealth lies in its flocks of sheep and herds of goats and camels.

However, the Bérabiche are not wholly given to raising flocks and herds, but carry on besides a very important salt trade with Timbuctoo. Not a day passes in this city but Bérabiche camels, laden with salt, arrive from the mines of Taodenni, and this highly profitable commerce is almost exclusively in the hands of this tribe.

Their constant dealings with Timbuctoo cause the Bérabiche to consider themselves as practically inhabitants of the city, where, in fact, they buy all the commodities they require. They are therefore obliged to come to the city, and for this reason have always had to subject themselves to the ruler of Timbuctoo.

For the rest, not only are all their most important interests in this town, but for half the year their flocks and herds live near its very walls. In summer only the herds of camels go into the Azaouad. In autumn they graze around Timbuctoo, and in the region of Hessiane, from Teneg-el-Haye to Rouzi.

At the present time their chief, a man of great influence, is Oueld-Mohemmed. The number of their tents may be estimated at 1500.

Usually the Bérabiche are armed with rifles and mounted on camels. Though not warlike, they have known how to preserve their liberty in the face of the Touareg, with whom, in certain places, they live. Now that they live in friendly relations with us, they greatly fear attacks from the Touareg ; they are also very much afraid of their enemies, the Allouch, and the Touareg of the north, the Hoggar, whose bands go on pillaging expeditions as far as Boudejebiha.

Kounta.—The Kounta are marabouts who formerly lived in Timbuctoo and its immediate neighbourhood. They exercised a strong religious influence over the city and over the Touareg of the region. This influence they have largely lost, owing to dissensions which arose between them and the Iguellad, and to their unavoidable struggles against the Toucouleurs. They have, therefore, almost entirely abandoned Timbuctoo.

They are now widely scattered, and are found in the region of Mabrouck to the north, in the Adrar to the east, and in the Aribinda to the south. They are mostly engaged in trade, and are no longer warriors.

The Kounta of the Aribinda, in whom we are particularly interested, wander over the country from the Lake Dô to the river.

They own many captives. These are separated into small groups, living in straw huts, and often moving their homes according to the requirements of agriculture, to which they devote themselves near the pools of the Haribongo region. Only two of these villages are permanent, Haribongo and Aghélal, and in them are found a considerable number of mud houses. Some of the Kounta, who have ceased to be nomads, live in the village of Haribongo.

The chief of the tribe, Arouata, lives in the Haribongo region.

CHAPTER V

OPERATIONS AGAINST THE TOUAREG

THE SITUATION AT THE TIME OF OUR ARRIVAL AT TIMBUCTOO

AMONG all these tribes the Touareg alone were our declared enemies. The Tengueriguif, the Iguellad, the Irreganaten and the Kel-Temoulaï were masters of the country, which they oppressed and pillaged. When we took possession of the country, and deprived them of the products which they had procured by these means, we naturally made them our foes ; and it was these tribes which must be conquered. The village people and the other nomad tribes took our side, timidly at first, then more and more openly as they became convinced by the establishment of our posts, that we were resolved to keep what we had conquered, and as we proved our superiority by the defeat of the Touareg.

Besides these four Touareg tribes, there were three others which had some military power and might have declared themselves our enemies ; these were the Bérabiche, the Igouadaren, and the Aouellimiden.

Bérabiche.—All the interests of the Bérabiche are in Timbuctoo. To forbid them access to the city and its neighbourhood would have been to deprive them of nearly all the necessities of life. As a matter of course they paid tribute to the rulers of Timbuctoo. Therefore, as soon as we arrived they placed themselves under our protection, and our relations with them have grown constantly more friendly. They supplied us with emissaries who, going into the various regions occupied by our enemies, brought back to us valuable and accurate information. They furnished us with thirty armed men in the expedition we made at the end of June against the Kel-Temoulaï.

Lastly, their chief, Oueld-Mehemmed, constantly exercised a pacifying influence upon the chiefs of the other tribes who had come to him for advice, especially upon Sekhaoui, chief of the Igouadaren.

Igouadaren.—This chief did, in fact, write us on February 24, by the advice and with the meditation of Oueld-Me-hemmed, asking us to make peace with him. After that his attitude became more friendly all the time. When the Irregana-ten and the Kel-Temoulaï urged him to ally himself with them to fight us he refused. He made the same answer to Ngouna, chief of the Iguellad, who at the end of May tried to form a coalition against us.

A merchant of Timbuctoo going to Boud-jebiha was robbed by some men of the Ter-banassen tribe, a group of the Igouadaren. At our request Sekhaoui caused the stolen goods to be found and restored to the merchant. He promised, furthermore, to do all in his power to prevent any such robberies in his territory for the future.

Aouellimiden.—This tribe is settled far from Timbuctoo. According to the vague information we had so far received, it seemed probable that they had no intention of dealing in any way with the tribes near that city. They had both water and pasturage in their own country, and did not depend in any way upon Timbuctoo.

From the military point of view, therefore, we had to do only with the four Touareg tribes that subsisted entirely upon Timbuctoo, and which were, in order of their importance, the Tengueriguif, the Iguellad, the Irreganaten, and the Kel-Temoulaï.

DESTRUCTION OF THE TOUAREG CAMP OF TAKAYEGOUROU

The chief of the village of Danga informed us that a band of Touareg Irreganaten was encamped at Takayegourou, on the right bank of the arm of the Niger which bounds the Island of Koura on the east : and that they were marshalling and repairing their pirogues in preparation for piracy on the river.

A small detachment under Captain Gautheron was sent to reconnoitre the place indicated, to drive away the bands in question, destroy their camps, and thus prevent them from pillaging.

The detachment was composed of one native sergeant, and 24 tirailleurs of the 6th company, one European sergeant and 20 tirailleurs of the 9th company, amounting altogether to 46 guns in pirogues, a barge armed with a machine gun, and commanded by a quartermaster, and three laptots[1] of the flotilla.

This little column reached Danga, on the Island of Koura, at 6.50 in the morning of 10th March. After staying for an hour in this village, in order to get further information about the places occupied by the Touareg, they arrived at Takayegourou at 9 in the morning. About a dozen Touareg horsemen were stationed on the sandhill behind which were their camps. A few volleys of musketry from our pirogues put them to flight.

Sergeant Dethire and 16 tirailleurs were left to guard the pirogues. Captain Gautheron landed with 28 tirailleurs and ascended

[1] Soudanese mariners.

K

the dune, at the foot of which he could see the three camps at Takayegourou which the Touareg with their flocks were already abandoning. Our rifle fire killed a few and scattered the rest. The camps were destroyed; and at 11.30 the detachment went up the arm of the Niger in our own crafts to search for the pirogues which the Touareg had been repairing. These were found in front of the Touareg camps at Inatane, which had been evacuated at the same time as those of Takayegourou. Both the pirogues and the camps were destroyed. Besides, all the animals captured which could not be carried in the pirogues were killed, viz. 10 horses, 42 asses, a few calves, and about 60 goats.

The Touareg, no longer feeling safe in this region, evacuated it. And the result of our expedition was to prevent the pillage about to be begun on the river.

This band was under the orders of El-Khadir, and belonged to the Irreganaten. As we found in their tents things which had belonged to Europeans of the Bonnier column and of the flotilla, such as a lantern, a coffee-pot, etc., we felt sure that they had taken part in the affair of Tacoubao, and our examination of the prisoners confirmed this.

EXPEDITION OF THE KILLI

One effect of the occupation of Goundam by our troops was to divide in two the Touareg of the left bank. On one hand were the Kel-Antassar, north of Goundam between Ras-el-Mâ and Farasch, and, near by, Sobo of the Tengueriguif tribe who, having been wounded on 15th January, could not go with his tribe, and had remained at Farasch with a few followers; on the other hand, the Tengueriguif who had passed the marigot of Goundam with their chief Mohammed-Ouel-Ouab and all their leading men. The latter were in the Killi and had appeared at Diré, about to embark in their pirogues for a piratical expedition on the river. They were also seen on the shores of the Lake of Fati, from which point they could either sack the villages of the Tioki, or rejoin the Kel-Antassar at Daouna

This was a favourable opportunity to put

an end to our troubles with this tribe, the most powerful and dreaded among the four tribes in the neighbourhood of Timbuctoo. The Killi is, in fact, accessible on all sides to pirouges, and it would be easy to guard all the passages by which the enemy, still in the Killi, could escape.

An operation · in combination with the post at Goundam was decided, and to this end the following instructions were sent to the commandant of Goundam:

" The courier who brings you this letter will give you a guide and two pirogues that will help you in crossing the marigot.

" You will leave Captain Philippe with half of his company and a platoon of Spahis at the post of Goundam. Captain Fourgeot and the section of mountain guns of 80 mm. will remain there also.

" You will take command of a column composed of 2 platoons of Spahis and half of the Philippe company. You will cross the marigot of Goundam in such manner that during the day of the 22nd you will leave its shore and reach Mory-Koïra before night, where I will wait for you.

" According to the guide whom I send you, there will be a marigot to cross about 5 miles from Goundam, and this will be the only troublesome passage you will have.

" Get all the information you can on your part, and if necessary take other guides at Goundam.

" If in any event you should not meet us, you will pass the night at Mory-Koïra. You will leave there on the 23rd to camp at Tondigamé, where you will find a platoon of tirailleurs in pirogues.

" My design is to go with one company in pirogues to Mory-Koïra ; there I will be on the 22nd to meet you. We shall thus have a chance of taking the Touareg between two fires. I will send a platoon in pirogues to Tondigomé, to prevent the Touareg from crossing the river.

" At Mory-Koïra or at Tondigamé you will find further instructions. If you find nothing there on the days herein specified, you will return to Goundam."

A column was organised at Timbuctoo under the orders of the lieutenant-colonel, as follows :

1. The Staff.
   Chief of Staff : Captain Cristofari.
   Surgeon : Dr. Lespinasse.
   Secretary : Sergeant Michel.
   Interpreter : Samba-Ibrahim.
   1 native orderly.
2. The 5th company of tirailleurs.
   Captain Puypéroux.
   Sub-lieutenant Bluzet (until the column should break up).
   1 native officer.
   5 European non-commissioned officers.
   1 European bugler.
   144 natives.
3. 1 platoon of the 10th company.
   Lieutenant Frèrejean.
   Native sub-lieutenant : Sadioka, who was to rejoin the platoon on its way through Kabara.
   4 European non-commissioned officers.
   75 natives.
4. The 27 tirailleurs of the 6th company who were at Kabara.
5. The barge armed with the machine-gun.

A letter from the commandant at Goundam, received on 18th March, informing us of the presence of the Touareg on the shores of the Lake of Fati, near and to the north of Mékoré, led to the following changes in the instructions which had been sent to him :

"I am just in receipt of your letter No. 5 of March 16th, and in accordance with the information it contains, I change the rendezvous given you in my letter No. 27, which you will receive by the same courier.

"I will be at Korango on the 23rd where I will land. On your part, reconnoitre the same day around Mékoré, with the troops indicated in my letter No. 27, in such manner that we can meet in that village on the 23rd.

"You will be notified of our presence by our guns if we have to shoot. If we do not have to shoot, I will order three volleys of musketry at midday, one minute apart.

"If by midday you have heard nothing, you will make arrangements to return to Goundam.

"In that case, I think you could pass the night without inconvenience at the old camp of Pouydebat."

The column, starting in the evening of the 18th from Timbuctoo, left Kabara in the morning of the 19th, and reached Koïrétago in the evening.

At the long halt on the 20th Captain Gautheron was left behind with all the large pirogues, one platoon of the 5th company, the detachment of the 6th company, the barge with the machine gun, the convoy and, in a word, everything which might retard our march. His instructions were to go to Diré, prevent the Touareg from crossing the river to join the Irreganaten, attempt to reach Lake Goro and be there, if possible, on the 24th to receive the Touareg whom the two columns from Goundam and Fati would drive back from this side.

He was to return to Diré on the 25th.

The column, now much more mobile, resumed its march at 2 o'clock in the afternoon. It was at Koura by 6 in the evening, where it halted for two hours, started again and reached Farabongo at 1 o'clock in the morning.

On the 21st the column started at 5 o'clock, made the long halt at Diré from 10 to 12, and stopped for two hours in the evening, from 7 to 9, on the right bank of the river opposite Safay. It continued

its march during the night and arrived
about 3 o'clock in the morning near Bala-
Maoundo.

On the 22nd the start was made at
6 o'clock, and the long halt at Tendirma
from 11 to 1. Then, after a long and
difficult trip over the high grass of the
Lake of Fati, it arrived at Mékoré at 3 in
the morning.

The village was immediately surrounded
by the 5th company. The inhabitants, who
made no attempt at flight, said that the
Touareg had left the region two days before
and were now in the Killi, around Godio.
Some fishermen captured the day before
confirmed this information.

In fact, during our march from Bala-
Maoundo to Tendirma, some signs of
movement had been noticed on the left
bank of the Issa-Ber.

On the 23rd the reconnoitring party from
Goundam joined the column at Mékoré at
7 in the morning. Captain Prost, commanding the reconnaissance, confirmed with
personal information the news already
known, that the Touareg were around Godio.

The following orders were given:

Captain Prost's column was to camp in the evening on the shore of Lake Fati, as near as possible to Goundam, and would get from there four days' rations. The next day, the 24th, it would march by land on Tendirma and Godio.

The river column was to retrace its steps, land near Bala-Maoundo, and march on the Touareg camps in the direction of Godio.

The first column left Mékoré at 8 o'clock, the second at 9 o'clock.

The river column arrived at 5 at Tendirma, where it passed the night.

Messengers from Ali-Habana had come to announce that this chief would visit the lieutenant-colonel very early the next morning.

On the morning of the 25th, Ali-Habana arrived at about 6 o'clock. A long palaver followed, Ali-Habana making strong protestations of friendship. He said that until that day a series of misunderstandings had prevented his coming to meet us, that he recognised our authority, and was ready to assist us.

He would send to the people of Godio, who were subject to him, news of our arrival, telling them not to run away, and to supply us with guides.

We left Tendirma at 11 in the morning.

From time to time sections of troops landed and explored the right bank of the Issa-Ber, following the shore for some distance, but nothing suspicious was reported.

Towards 3 o'clock the laptot quartermaster, Bakary-Cissé, came in a pirogue with a letter from Captain Gautheron, who reported as follows:

"We arrived at Diré ruins 22nd March, at 7 in the morning, in a reconnaissance of the surrounding country. A pirogue which fled at our approach, led to our discovery of the entrance into the marigot which leads to the lake of Goro. We entered this marigot with three small pirogues to reconnoitre. We found that there was very little water, and navigation was very difficult. Therefore, leaving the barge with the machine-gun, 12 tirailleurs, and the convoy at the entrance, we went on to the marigot with three small pirogues and one large one, which I was obliged to have carried, so to speak, by the bozos and the tirailleurs.

"At 4.30 we landed near the camp of Dahouré, and there surprised the Touareg, who fled at the first shots, leaving several men on the ground.

"The tabala sounded all the night of the 22nd–23rd, from a northerly direction.

"At 6.30 in the morning of the 23rd, Captain Gautheron commenced a march in that direction; at 7 o'clock he reached a sandhill, on top of which were stationed warriors of the enemy. He opened fire on them; they returned the fire very unskil- fully, with guns taken from us at Tacoubao; then, having advanced slowly to within 150 metres of the tirailleurs, they made a vigorous charge. Our volleys stopped them and put them to flight, but some of them fell less than 15 metres from us.

"The pursuit of them was continued for nearly 4 miles.

"No losses on our side, Sergeant Cassinet of the 5th company alone being slightly wounded in the hand by a ricochet.

"The Touareg left more than 60 dead

on the ground, among them being their principal chiefs: Mohammed-Oueld-Ouab, Mody, Atta, Tereseti, etc.

"The spoils were 9 rapid-firing rifles of the 1874 and 1884 models, 2 bayonets, 1 officer's revolver, about 1000 cartridges, stripes of a lieutenant-colonel, a field-glass, a surgeon's case, tirailleurs' uniforms, etc.

"Forty horses, 80 camels, 150 asses, 20 oxen, 100 sheep, which could not be carried away, were killed on the spot."

When this letter arrived the column had halted on the bank of the river, not far from Bala-Maoundo.

The defeat of the Touareg near Goro emboldened the people of the neighbouring villages, who came to bring us the news and offer themselves as guides to other camps. From the various information they gave us we gathered that the Touareg were all together at Sansan with their flocks, and were about to start for the Lake of Daouna, passing between Lake Fati and Goundam.

A letter was therefore sent by two couriers to Captain Prost to inform him of these facts.

The column then went to Diédou, where it was joined in the evening by Naval Lieutenant Boiteux. At 1 in the morning, leaving Lieutenant Boiteux and a small detachment of tired or sick tirailleurs to guard the pirogues, the column marched for Sansan. After a very hard night march, three-quarters of the time over the muddy bottoms of the marigots, it arrived at 7 in the morning before the camps, from which it was still separated by a last, large marigot about 4 feet deep and over 880 yards wide, and which it took more than half an hour to cross.

The Touareg, who had seen us, fled precipitately. By the time the column reached the other side of the marigot, the abandoned flocks were wandering in every direction, and tents rolled up and ready to be taken away were left as they were, as well as other bundles of small articles and of food ready to be eaten.

A section of the 10th company, under Lieutenant Frèrejean, formed at the left, the platoon of the 5th company, under Captain Puypéroux at the right, and one section of the 10th company in reserve. In this formation the march was begun. In about fifteen minutes the two sections in advance opened fire, and Captain Puypéroux, who had spread his men over the right bank, fired on a band of Touareg and drove them back to Lieutenant Frèrejean. The pursuit was actively continued until 9.30, at which time the Touareg were beyond effective reach of our guns, and distant firing showed that they had fallen on the Prost column. At noon a letter came from Captain Prost saying that, convinced there was nothing more to do at Godio, on hearing our fire he had moved towards us. He reported the capture the previous day of 40 prisoners and a herd of 400 oxen. Between the Lake of Fati and Goundam he had come upon the band defeated on the 23rd by Captain Gautheron.

Soon after, Lieutenant Frantz (11th company), of the Prost detachment, joined the column with his platoon.

He reported that he had met the Touareg dispersed by us fleeing towards the Lake of Fati, and that he had pursued and fired upon them.

The column passed the night on the spot. Next day the platoon of the 10th company convoyed to Goundam the herd of sheep, goats and asses captured at Sansan. The lieutenant-colonel, with the platoon of the 5th company, returned to Diédou, arriving there at noon and leaving again in pirogues at 2 o'clock. Captain Gautheron rejoined the column on his way to Diré on the 27th. He reported that on 25th March he had captured 13 suspected pirogues which were trying to cross the river, and taken prisoners the 34 men who were in them. The column arrived at Kabara on the 28th at 10 in the morning, and at Timbuctoo at 2 o'clock.

During these operations we had two wounded: one European,[1] Sergeant Cassinet with a scratch on the hand, and one native Spahi with three lance cuts.

The Tengueriguif left 120 dead on the field. Ten guns and one revolver, taken by the Touareg on 15th January at Tacoubao, fell into our hands. We captured or killed

[1] Joffre himself.

50 horses, 30 camels, 8000 sheep, 400 oxen, and 200 asses.

Nearly all the chiefs were killed, and the tribe of the Tengueriguif could be considered as destroyed. The remnants of them went to Ras-el-Mâ, near the Iguellad.

The Tengueriguif were the most powerful Touareg tribe of the four living around Timbuctoo. It was they who, along with a small band of Irreganaten, made the attack at Tacoubao. Their destruction had a considerable effect throughout the country, and the results were felt in the submission of non-combatant tribes, and in the increased loyalty of the tribes and villages which had already submitted to us.

THE SUBMISSION OF THE COUNTRY

In fact, after the foregoing operations, the following tribes came to Timbuctoo, with their submission:

The Cheurfiga (chiefs: Boukri and Alfaka).

The Ahl-Aouza (chief: Saïd-Ben-Faki).

The Imededghen, vassals of the Tengueri-guif (chief: Mohammed-Oueld-Touhami).

The Kel-Inchéria (chief: Ben-Doudou).

L

The Kel-Es-Souk.

The Kel-Nekounder (chief: Djeddou).

The Ahk-Sidi-Ali had already submitted to our authority on 11th March.

Only three of all the nomad tribes of the region were still unsubdued, the Iguellad, the Irreganaten and the Kel-Temoulaï. The Tengueriguif, reduced to a small number of tents and having no more value as a fighting force, sent emissaries to us on two different occasions to demand *aman*.[1] They have not yet followed up these overtures, although each time they received a favourable reply.

As to the stationary population, they had placed themselves under our authority from the time of our arrival at Timbuctoo.

Two meetings of their leading men were held on 22nd and 24th February. They nominated as chief of the city Alfa-Saïdou, who had assumed the duties of this office since the arrival of Naval Lieutenant Boiteux. Alfa-Saïdou belonged to the group of the Tolba, and was a very active and

---

[1] To demand *aman* is to ask for peace. The phrase is used by all the Arab-speaking tribes.

influential man, entirely devoted to the French cause.

The city was divided into two quarters; the western part Djengueri-Ber, with Ben-Ali-Moussoudou, of the Rouma, as chief; and the eastern part Saré-Kaina, with San-Oueld-El-Kaïd-Boubeker, also of the Rouma, as chief.

Aoussa-Katawal.—This canton, evacuated by the Iguellad on the passage of our column, submitted. The chief men followed the column as far as Timbuctoo, where we confirmed the authority of their chief, Sididio.

But after our establishment at Timbuctoo a few bands of Iguellad returned to the upper region of the lakes situated north of this canton, a district too far away for us to be able to give it prompt and adequate protection, and one night some of them assassinated the chief Sididio in his straw hut in the village of Katawal.

The inhabitants of the north of the canton could not avoid complying with the demands of their former masters. To protect and govern this country efficiently it seemed indispensable, therefore, to set up a centre of government at Soumpi, to fill the much too extensive void between Goundam and Sokolo.

Soboundou-Samba. — The chief of the canton of Nioukou-Alfa-Guidalo, who had resisted us when our column went to Nia-founké, sent a party of his leading men to Timbuctoo on 28th March to bring his submission.

Tioki.—As we have already seen, Ali-Habana came to Tendirma during the operations in the Killi, to tender his submission.

Killi.—All the villages of the Killi surrendered after the operations in March.

Kissou.—Those of the Kissou submitted at the time of the column's arrival before Goundam in the beginning of February.

Fitouka.—Lastly, Omar-Abdallah-Galawal, chief of the Fitouka, who had rebelled against any idea of submission, and had refused to recognise the authority of Agui-bou, sent some of his chief men to Timbuctoo on 28th March, to bring his submission, which was accepted.

Expedition against the Irreganaten

In April, a party of Irreganaten crossed the river in front of Danga during the night, and pillaged that village. After this act of brigandage all the Irreganaten assembled on the right bank a little to the east of Iloua.

This assemblage at a point so near Timbuctoo was threatening to the tribes and villages which had surrendered to us. It was necessary to disperse the Irreganaten to avoid a repetition of such brigandage as had occurred at Danga.

A marching column was organised under the direct command of the lieutenant-colonel, which comprised the 9th company under Captain Pansier, one platoon of the 10th company under Lieutenant Maillac, and 10 Spahis under Lieutenant Robillot.

The column left Timbuctoo on 21st April, at 4.50 in the afternoon, embarked in pirogues at Kabara, left that post at 9.30 in the evening, and reached Iloua on the 22nd at 3.20 in the morning.

It left Iloua at 4 in the morning, taking

four guides there. The pirogues left the Niger to follow a channel in the middle of the inundations, and from this time navigation became very difficult over the high grasses which entirely covered the sheet of water.

We learned on the way, at about 7.30 in the morning, from two fishermen of Bourem, that the previous day the Touareg had left the camps we had planned to attack, and were then at Aghélal.

At 11.45 the column halted on the river, east of the Lake of Ouékoré, about 7 miles from Aghélal, and camped at that point. A few natives were sent in a pirogue in the direction of Aghélal to reconnoitre the position of the enemy's camps. They returned at 6 in the evening with two prisoners who were to guide us that same night to the camps.

The column started again on the 22nd at 11 o'clock at night. It reached Aghélal on the 23rd at 6 in the morning, navigation being very slow on account of the high grass.

A section of the 9th company, commanded

by Adjutant Sistach, stayed behind to guard
the pirogues and the convoy.

The column landed and marched for an
hour through muddy marshes, arriving about
7.30 at a point near the Touareg camps,
which had been hurriedly evacuated. The
Touareg had left a part of their baggage
behind. Some distance away we could see
a cloud of thick dust which showed where
the numerous flocks were running in all directions. We went after the fleeing Touareg,
but as the pursuit led us into regions where
there is no water, it was stopped at 9.30.

We returned to the pirogues with 35
prisoners, and the column reached Kabara
on the 25th at 7 in the morning, and Timbuctoo at 10, without having had any losses.

The Touareg who, to escape our pursuit,
had fled with their flocks into a region
where there is absolutely no water, and
where they remained a long time, suffered
greatly from thirst. About a hundred of
them died, and they lost many cattle.

After this expedition the Irreganaten and
the Kel-Temoulaï assembled and went east-
ward to ask protection of Sekhaoui, chief of

the Igouadaren.   This chief replied that he
was allied with the French, and did not
wish to deceive them, and that if they
wanted to live in peace the only thing for.
them to do was to surrender.

OPERATIONS AGAINST THE IGUELLAD

On 9th April a few Kel-Antassar fell
upon a herd of 80 oxen entrusted to the
village of Goundam and grazing 3 miles to
the north of it.   They killed the two herds-
men, and drove the herd to the north of
the Lake of Faguibine.   On the 10th a
reconnoitring party consisting of 50 tirailleurs and 20 Spahis started under the orders
of Lieutenant Frantz to search the country
between the mountain and Lake Télé.   At
the same time, a platoon of Spahis followed
the eastern side of the mountain as far
as the defile of Karao-Kamba.

The reconnoitring party found a camp
of Kel-Antassar, killed nine men, made 17
prisoners, and returned to Goundam the
same evening.

During the latter half of April and all

of May the Iguellad were quiet. Most of them, as well as nearly all their chiefs, wanted peace.

Loudegh, brother of Ngouna,[1] wrote to us to ask for a man; and Oueld-Mehemmed, chief of the Bérabiche, sent an emissary to Ngouna urging him to stop a war the issue of which could only be fatal to him. But Ngouna, feeling that his tribe was deserting him, inveighed against his brother with great violence for having made overtures of submission, and tried to organise a coalition of the Touareg tribes against us. The emissary whom he sent for this purpose to Sekhaoui, chief of the Igouadaren, was coldly received by the latter. Assalmi, chief of the Irreganaten, would not listen to these proposals either.

Under these circumstances, Ngouna, able to count only upon a small number of Kel-Antassar warriors, tried to compromise the entire tribe and to break off all peace negotiations. With this object, in the night of 27th–28th May, about a hundred Kel-Antassar, mounted on camels, left

[1] Chief of the Kel-Antassar, Iguellad warriors.

Farasch and arrived before dawn at the village of Dongoï. They killed 14 inhabitants, including the chief of the village, wounded two others, and returned to Farasch with such booty as they could get and a few prisoners.

Already, on the morning of the 27th, a few Kel-Antassar had come down the mountain and surprised some of the inhabitants of Goundam just as they were beginning to work in their fields on the shore of the Lake of Télé, 8 km. from the village. They carried off six and killed two who would not go with them.

On the 28th Captain Bigaut had sent a party, commanded by Captain Laperrine, to reconnoitre the shores of the lake and find and destroy the camp from which these pillagers had probably come.

On receiving news of the brigandage committed at Dongoï. Captain Bigaut had sent Captain Laperrine orders to push his reconnaissance as far as possible and cut off the retreat of the Kel-Antassar.

Captain Laperrine passed the night with his party at Karao-Kamba, and resumed his

march on the morning of the 29th. At
7.30 he found at Kameina camel tracks
coming from the direction of Dongoï, which
he followed as far as Sakénébaga, where he
arrived at 11.30 in the morning.

The Kel-Antassar who were at Sakénébaga, warned by their captives, had time to
mount their camels and flee.   However,
they left 20 prisoners with us, and had to
abandon a part of their plunder, while the
people from Goundam and Dongoï whom
they had carried off were able to make their
escape.

The reconnoitring party were back at
Goundam on the 31st, at 8 in the morning.

The Combat of Fati.—At the time of the
pillage of Dongoï, Ngouna had ordered
another inroad upon the region of the Killi.
This occurred in the night of 8th-9th June
at Ougoukoré, a village situated about
5 miles north of Sansan.   Seventy Iguellad,
commanded by Djeddou, set out from
Daouna, fell upon Ougoukoré, and completely pillaged it.   The inhabitants fled
into the bush and sent a warning to
Goundam.

Captain Bigaut sent, under command of Captain Gérard, a platoon of the 10th Soudanese company and 16 Spahis to the north of the mountain of Fati where the Iguellad would have to pass on their way back to Daouna.

After having crossed the marigot of Goundam and covered 2½ miles, the detachment found two parallel tracks a few yards apart, one made by camels, the other by men. Here evidently the Iguellad had passed on their way to Ougoukoré, and as it was not unlikely that they would return by the same road, native Sub-lieutenant Sadioka, with his section and two Spahis, was stationed in ambush behind a small hillock near the tracks. Meanwhile the remainder of the detachment continued its march nearly to the Lake of Fati to intercept the enemy in case he took the second road which lies between the lake and the mountain.

The latter troops had hardly reached their destination when, at about noon, the Sadioka section saw the Iguellad arrive, laden with booty. The tirailleurs, without being seen, stationed themselves in a line

on the ridge of the hillock, and they did
not shoot until the enemy were within easy
range. At the first firing a few men were
hit; whereupon the others dismounted from
their camels, made the animals kneel down,
and prepared to charge on our tirailleurs.
The latter advanced quickly and dispersed
the Iguellad in every direction, but chiefly
towards the mountain. Captain Gérard,
who had run up at the first reports of our
rifles, was in time to fire on the band that
was fleeing to the mountain, while the
Spahis charged and killed a few.

The enemy were now in full flight, leaving
45 dead on the field. All the booty carried
off by the Touareg was restored to the
Ougoukoré people, and nine camels were
taken to Goundam as well as two captured
rifles, model of 1874.

This defeat terrified the Touareg. After
that, both the Iguellad and Kel-Antassar
remained quiet.

From their camps around the Lake of
Fagnibine, the Touareg, at the time of
writing, starting from Daouna or from
Farasch, can still make raids into the Tioki,

the Killi and the Kissou. Mounted on camels they can cover great distances in the night, and fall unexpectedly on villages far from their camps, which they pillage, generally making their escape before the post at Goundam can receive warning or have time to send troops effectively. As long as the Iguellad are not driven from the shores of the Lake of Fagnibine, or do not surrender, the populations of certain villages north of the Tioki, of the Killi and the Kissou, will have no peace.

To subdue this tribe it would be necessary to have a column patrol around the lake for twenty or thirty days, but on account of the great heat and the tornadoes this cannot be undertaken in summer, though it could be easily done from October onward.

At the time of writing it was believed that the following measures ensured peace to the country, and enabled the inhabitants to go on with their farming:

Four temporary posts had been installed between Timbuctoo aud Goundam, at Tassakant, El-Massara, Douékéré, and Djinjin.

They were protected by a thick thorn hedge, and contained straw shelters. Small detachments of troops could pass the night there without fear of surprise, and could have shelter from the heat during the day. Detachments could thus pass to and fro without fatigue between Goundam and Timbuctoo, and prevent bands of Iguellad from making raids on the Killi and the Kissou.

Furthermore, the post of Goundam had a sufficient number of pirogues to transport a platoon of infantry. Therefore, when warned of a Touareg camp on the shore of the lake, it could land a force strong enough to destroy it. The Iguellad watered their flocks and had valuable farms on the shores of these lakes. It was a vulnerable point where the post of Goundam could inflict much damage without over-fatiguing the troops.

EXPEDITION AGAINST THE KEL-TEMOULAÏ

Although Assalmi, chief of the Irreganaten, had refused with an evasion the advances of Ngouna, and though up to this time the Kel-Temoulaï had always made common cause with the Irreganaten, about 50 Kel-Temoulaï crossed the river at Billasao on 20th June, and at 8 in the evening attacked a Bérabiche camp a few kilometres north-east of Kabara. They captured a thousand sheep and killed about ten men. The post of Kabara, warned at 1 o'clock, sent at 2 in the morning 20 Spahis and a band of Bérabiche to chase the plunderers. They could not catch them; but the Kel-Temoulaï, fleeing rapidly from their pursuers, left half of the stolen sheep behind, and these were re-taken by the Bérabiche.

After this incursion it was necessary to teach the Kel-Temoulaï a lesson, first, to prevent their repeating it, and then to strengthen our relations with the Bérabiche, who had hitherto rendered us valuable services and could do us many more in the future.

A column composed of the 5th Soudanese company, 20 Spahis and 80 Bérabiche armed with rifles, was placed under the command of Captain Puypéroux. The first section, comprising a platoon of infantry, the 20

Spahis and 80 Bérabiche, under Sub-lieutenant Bluzet, left Kabara on the 26th, at 4 in the morning, and went to Billasao to pass the night. The second section (1 platoon of infantry) under the direct orders of Captain Puypéroux, left in pirogues at noon of the same day. The two sections met at Billasao.

The crossing of the Niger began on the 27th at 5 in the morning in the pirogues which had been bought, and was finished at 7 o'clock. The column then started, guided by the Bérabiche. At noon, near Aghélal, they came upon the Kel-Temoulaï camps which had been suddenly abandoned. The pursuit was begun, the Spahis chasing the fleeing enemy, and the Bérabiche picking up the booty and other things of which large quantities had been left behind; 16 Touareg were killed, and about 100 taken prisoners.

As the enemy were now scattered in the bush in all directions, they could not be reached, and the column camped 2 miles east of Aghélal. At 9 in the evening, after a heavy tornado, a party of Touareg horsemen were seen prowling around our camp. They

M

were received with rifle shots. Two of them came right up to the thorn hedge which enclosed our camp. One was unhorsed and his mount taken; the other, who was the chief of the Kel-Temoulaï, succeeded in escaping.

The column left on the 27th at 7 in the morning. It recrossed the river at Billasao and reached Timbuctoo in the evening of the 28th. A large part of the booty was distributed among the Bérabiche to compensate them for the losses the Kel-Temoulaï had caused them in the night of the 20–21st.

It seemed probable that the Touareg of the right bank—the Irreganaten and the Kel-Temoulaï—would make no further inroads of this kind, at least for some time. To make it more difficult for them, the barges of the flotilla were kept at Koriumé, where, furthermore, they were needed during the summer to protect the pirogues of Timbuctoo. At any moment when news might come of a band of Touareg crossing the river, it would suffice to send one or two barges, which were always kept in readiness to capture pillaging pirogues, and thus cut off their retreat. As the Touareg require some time to prepare a sudden attack, 24 hours at least, the barges could generally be sent in time, and the Touareg, knowing this, would probably keep quiet.

CHAPTER VI

RIVER COMMUNICATION

THE river communication with Mopti is
ensured by the posts of El-Oualedji, Saraféré and Gourao.

The post of El-Oualedji, about 22 miles
from Goundam, connects the latter with the
river. From this point opposite Safay,
both arms of the Niger can be watched.
This post which, for the moment, was rather
far from all the centres of habitation had
required much labour and initiative on the
part of Captain Philippe, who had charge of
the work. The strong thorn hedge which
protected it and the straw huts for lodging
the Europeans and natives were finished, at
the time of writing.

Saraféré is a place of great importance.
It is a commercial centre through which
pass nearly all the food products sent for the

provisioning of Timbuctoo, and of the tribes that buy their food in the city. Captain Gautheron had fitted up a group of village houses and placed them temporarily in a state of defence. This work was then completed, but, winter being past, it would be necessary to build a post.

TELEGRAPHIC COMMUNICATION

At the time of writing the telegraph line of Kayes stopped at Ségou, and telegrams had to be carried in pirogues from Ségou to Timbuctoo. This journey never required less than ten days, and usually 12. This was a great inconvenience which it was necessary to remedy as soon as possible.

On account of the inundations of the river, it was impossible to construct an aerial telegraph line near the Niger. Such a line would have to skirt the flooded lands. If we wanted to install the line on the right bank, it would be necessary, before reaching Timbuctoo, to cross the Niger which in the rainy season is 25 miles wide in this part. That way was therefore impracticable.

M 2

The only possible course would lie on the left bank, generally following the road taken by the Joffre column, and skirting to the north the lakes which are fed by the Niger floods. But this line would run through vast uninhabited regions which were at that time very unsafe, and in which we could neither construct the telegraph nor efficiently guard it until the tribes north of Diartou, Soumpi and Goundam were conquered.

For the moment another solution had to be sought, and it seemed that the system of visual signalling would furnish it. El-Oualedji was visible from the mountain of Goundam. Possibly Saraféré could be seen also, or at any rate the highest part of a dune near by. From Saraféré we could communicate with the mountain of Lake Dhébo by means of one or more intervening posts. Finally, from this mountain we could see the mountain of Bandiagara, and there find the necessary intermediate points to connect with Ségou.

Topographical Service

An order had been given for two maps to be made at each post, one at 1/100,000, of the environs of the post, drawn from the reports of different reconnoitring parties; the other, at 1/500,000, of the region, founded on information procured for the purpose.

Owing to our lack of draughtsmen, and other means, it had not been possible to carry out this order at that time except at Timbuctoo. Sub-lieutenant Bluzet, who was entrusted with the work, had now been able to make a map of the region with the help of itineraries and numerous reconnaissances made, both by land and water, from Timbuctoo and from Goundam, and from various informations gathered at these two posts. This map, though still imperfect, gave an accurate idea of the country from the political as well as topographical point of view. The two plans reprinted in the present report, were founded on the work of Sub-lieutenant Bluzet.

The Situation on 10th July, 1894

On the 10th July the situation was as follows :

From the military point of view, the posts which had been created were well on the way to completion, and were all in a state of defence.

From the political point of view, the entire stationary population of the region had submitted. Among the nomads, the Bérabiche and Kounta on one hand, the Igouadaren, and all the small Berber tribes on the other, had recognised our authority. The submission of these different tribes extended our sphere of influence as far as the country beyond Araouane, through the Bérabiche, and 155 miles east of Timbuctoo through the Igouadaren and the Kounta, that is to say as far as the Falls of Tosaye.

The four Touareg tribes which had fought us — the Tengueriguif, Irreganaten, Kel-Temoulaï and Iguellad—were not yet entirely submissive to our rule. Nevertheless, the Tengueriguif, almost annihilated, had tried to find out on several occasions whether their overtures of submission would not be well received.   At the time of writing, their emissaries had just come to Timbuctoo to make proposals for peace.

The chief of the Irreganaten, after having first tried to send the Kounta, then Aguibou, as emissaries, finally wrote direct to Timbuctoo to demand *aman*.

The Kel-Temoulaï, who are few in number, and have joined fortunes with the Irreganaten, will probably follow the lead of the latter by submitting.

As for the Iguellad, they had remained quiet since their defeat at Fati on 9th June. The entire tribe wanted peace.   Under these circumstances it was probable that Oueld-Mehemmed, chief of the Bérabiche, would persuade Ngouna, the only advocate of war, to surrender.   Nevertheless, measures were taken for the protection of the tribes which had submitted against any inroads that might be attempted by the Kel-Antassar.

Printed in the United States
142072LV00003B/163/A